The Audacious Woman:

Blaze Your Own Path to Prosperity

2nd Edition

Pamela Y. Toussaint, MBA

with

Tamara Toussaint, JD

Copyright © 2018 Pamela Y. Toussaint. All rights reserved. No portion of this book may be reproduced mechanically, electronically, or by any other means, including photocopying, without written permission of the publisher. It is illegal to copy this book, post it to a website, or distribute it by any other means without permission from the publisher.

Pamela Y. Toussaint
P.O. 211842
West Palm Beach, Florida 33411
561-632-8672
Pamela@UltimateImageCoach.com
http://www.UltimateImageCoach.com

Second Edition
ISBN-13-978-1985569867
ISBN-10-1985569868
ASIN: B079SL5S97 (Amazon Kindle)

First Edition
ISBN-13: 978-1508817369
ISBN-10: 1508817367
ASIN: B00VWA297Y (Amazon Kindle)

Limits of Liability and Disclaimer of Warranty

The author and publisher shall not be liable for your misuse of this material. This book is strictly for informational and educational purposes.

Warning–Disclaimer

The purpose of this book is to educate and entertain. The author and/or publisher do not guarantee that anyone following these techniques, suggestions, tips, ideas, or strategies will become successful. The author and/or publisher shall have neither liability nor responsibility to anyone with respect to any loss or damage caused, or alleged to be caused, directly or indirectly by the information contained in this book.

DEDICATION

This book is dedicated to my mother, Vioris Cynthia Scott (1919-1997), who is the greatest inspiration to my siblings, my children, me, and everyone whose paths she crossed. Newly widowed with five children, ages 12 and younger, yet a fearless entrepreneur and role model who wore many hats, Vioris Scott was wise and generous beyond words; and made no mistake about her priority—her family. She taught by example to live a no-limits life. Hard work, optimism, out-of-the–box thinking, creating new paths, and kindness were her brand attributes. Oh, yes, my mother was the ***ultimate audacious woman***!

TABLE OF CONTENTS

TESTIMONIALS 6
ACKNOWLEDGMENTS 13
PROLOGUE 16

CHAPTER 1 -
FROM CAREER TRANSITION TO LIFE
TRANSFORMATION 29

CHAPTER 2 -
THE AUDACITY TO DREAM & IMAGINE PROSPERITY 46

CHAPTER 3 -
FIND YOUR PERSONAL BRAND SWEET SPOT 58

CHAPTER 4 -
DIFFERENTIATE AND DISRUPT 70

CHAPTER 5 -
RADIATE A POWERFUL IMAGE 89

CHAPTER 6 -
STAND UP! SPEAK UP! POWER UP! 101

CHAPTER 7 -
THE AUDACITY TO DISRUPT THE STATUS QUO 116

CHAPTER 8 -
BUILD IT BEFORE YOU NEED IT 130

EPILOGUE -
LOVE, LAUGH, PROSPER! **137**

ABOUT THE AUTHORS 146
CONNECT WITH PAMELA & TAMARA 149
REFERENCE & READING LIST 150

TESTIMONIALS

"My first thought when I read about the audacity to disrupt the status quo, was WOW, which means Words of Wisdom. I wished this was the start of a new book, I wanted more. The content is relevant, current and practical, specifically the short and long-term approaches to disrupt the status quo. In our current economic and social climate, Fake news and real abuse is common place. This chapter serves as a recap of the disruption of our society, and workplace while arming us with the tools to tangible transformation. I have received the call to action and will utilize the tools such as Build Entrepreneurial Skills and the GAEN network."

Ann McLaughlin
Author, Professor, Entrepreneur

"Pamela Toussaint walks her talk. She is an AWE-dacious woman with the passion, experience, and authority to write this inspiring book. And thank goodness that she has because we can all benefit from her wisdom and expertise. Self-esteem, a sense

of purpose, and the courage to face adversity are foundational cornerstones to living a meaningful and satisfying life... one that leads to the prosperity that we each deserve. Read this book, be inspired, and own your power NOW."

~ Minx Boren
Master Certified Coach, Motivational Speaker, Poet & Author of *Healing Is a Journey; Feeling My Way;* and *Soul Notes*

"Even though Jamaica was recently highlighted as leading the world in proportion of women managers, we have a long way to go. Our talented women need to focus on owning their power and achieving success in senior leadership positions and as entrepreneurs. The Audacious Woman is a call to action for women across the world to take charge of their future by implementing the personal branding strategies outlined in the book."

~ Sandra Scott
Deputy Director of Tourism, Marketing
Jamaica Tourist Board

"I was always taught that a person is their word, and this certainly rings true for my experience of Pamela Toussaint. Her own audaciousness radiates from her, and how she shows up in life is her greatest testimonial. For those who have yet to experience her directly, this book does the job."

~ Rev. Taylor E. Stevens
Senior Minister
Unity of the Palm Beaches

"You are smarter than you think and stronger than you look. So take a chance on yourself and others will take a chance with you. In The Audacious Woman, *Pamela inspires women, from college students to baby boomers, to take control of their careers, stand out, and implement bold actions."*

~ Dr. Maria Vallejo
Provost, Palm Beach State College, Lake Worth Campus

"If you want to step into your greatness, you will absolutely want to read The Audacious Woman: Blaze Your Own Path to Prosperity.

Pamela Toussaint's book isn't just about up-leveling your brand. It is so much more. It will literally transform your life. You just have to be willing to take the next steps and read this book now!"

~ AmondaRose Igoe
6-Figure Speaking Goddess and Award Winning Speaking Expert

"A genuine belief in one's capability is a fundamental criterion for success. I've met so many women with innovative and economically viable business ideas, yet their success is inhibited by lack of self-belief. If we start with the premise that we are much more capable than we would give ourselves credit for, then anything is possible. So go ahead, own your future, develop a road map, change gears and scale heights you never thought possible. The Audacious Woman *provides a personal branding guide that inspires women to own their power and transform their careers and lives."*

~ Cheryl Gowdie
BA (Hons.), FCIPD, MBA, CBC™
Accezy Coaching & Consulting Co.

"Few of us are brave enough to transform our careers, our lives, and our outlooks. Fortunately, Pamela Toussaint not only did just that, but she was also conscientious enough to share the process with other women who are ready to make a big change in their lives. The pages of The Audacious Woman *are the next best thing to having a life coach or mentor."*
~ Marilyn Murray Willison
Motivational Speaker, Author of *The Self-Empowered Woman* and *One Woman, Four Decades, Eight Wishes*

"Pam has taken her advocacy on women's empowerment to a new level taking on abuse and harassment issues. She lays out a compelling path for women and men to co-create a future whose hallmarks are mutual respect and prosperity."
CaraJoy Nash
MBA, Private Tutor, Social Media Expert
ShesOnline.media

"I meet women every day who aspire to become entrepreneurs but find it daunting to walk away from a steady paycheck. They cite the lack of female mentors, role models and a guide

book to help them have the confidence to make the leap. The Audacious Woman *provides practical advice that gives the aspiring female entrepreneur confidence to take that bold step and strike out on her own!"*

~ Natalie Madeira Cofield
President & CEO of the Greater Austin
Black Chamber of Commerce
Founder, *Walker's Legacy*

"Pamela Toussaint writes about her dedication to women's success with utmost passion and commitment. She sees individual branding as the roadway to personal insight and professional accomplishment. Her book is encouraging, heartfelt and hopeful for those wanting to change their destiny. Toussaint reassures her readers that anything is possible and that we have the capability to transform. With her prescriptive steps to branding and self-reflection, you are reassured that anyone can have their ideal career and life by being bold and stepping out."

~ Dr. Jean A. Wihbey
Palm Beach State College
Provost-Palm Beach Garden

"Being born to a family of women who were more than equal, feminism—without even formulating the word, or the concept for that matter—was a given, a self-evident truth. My sister, Pamela, eloquently shares how our mother's legacy has shaped the adults we've become—The recognition of which has established my value system, and informed my behavior and outlook throughout my entire life."

~ Kurt P. Scott
Director of Renewable Energy,
Business Development
Global Manager, Solar Energy
Competence Center
Atlas Material Testing Technology LLC

ACKNOWLEDGMENTS

My Husband

My husband, Gabriel, without whose love and support I would not, and could not, have embarked on and completed this journey. He has been urging me to write a book for many decades. He is the strongest accountability partner one could ever have. Thanks, Gabe, for your patience, love and persistence, for proof-reading many drafts, and for always telling me, "You are an excellent writer, you should write a book." Guess what "WE DID IT!"

Our Children

Gabriel Jr. is the "idea and words" man. Whenever I struggle with how to position and say something, he picks the right words with such ease. Gabriel Jr. is the ultimate marketing mind. He pushes me to think of *Ultimate Image Coach* and the far-reaching impact it can have on women and men globally.

Tamara, my co-author and *Ultimate Image Coach* partner, has stretched me to explore what's possible in our business. She has extended our personal branding consulting and training business to appeal to millennial professionals and other key demographics and professions. She exemplifies the power of networking and polished image.

My Siblings

Andree, Patricia, Sandra, and Kurt, even though our career paths have taken us across continents and rarely living in the same place, we remain a tight-knit family. Our love and support for each other has strengthened our bond and prosperity. We have all overcome many obstacles and succeeded in our careers and lives—testament to the traits our mother instilled in us.

Contributors, Reviewers, and Endorsers

Thanks to all of my friends, colleagues, and mentors who have encouraged me along this journey, reviewed my drafts, and provided testimonials. The journey has been a marathon, and you have been there to pick me up and encourage me to the finish line.

Editor and Collaborator

Thanks to my Awesome Editor and Friend, Peggy Lee Hanson, who guided and encouraged me along the way. Her expertise, warm, and encouraging personality gave me the push I needed to stay on track and stay focused. Peggy, you entered my journey at just the right time and for that I say a huge Thank You.

The journey continues.

I love you all!

PROLOGUE

"There is no more liberating, no more exhilarating experience than to determine one's position, state it bravely and then act."
~ Eleanor Roosevelt, *Eleanor Roosevelt, Volume One 1884-1933*[1]

I quit my Human Resources (HR) executive job in August 2010. I took a bold step to re-write my life's story by re-branding myself as *The Ultimate Image Coach*. I walked away from a six-figure salary and a 40-year career to pursue my passion. I did not make this decision lightly. I had always known that I wanted to do more and use my God-given talents and expertise to help others succeed in their professional and personal lives. I just didn't know when I would make the leap and what I would ultimately do.

I was not known to be a risk-taking entrepreneur. Prior to launching out on my own, I had been a classic "conformist"—a corporate professional. A steady paycheck and benefits made me feel safe. I had a family to support, bills to pay and loved to take nice vacations. I had been lulled into a false sense of security and fulfillment.

However, looking back, I realized that my improbable, audacious entrepreneurial journey began many decades ago. You might say it was in my DNA.

I was born and raised in a small village in Jamaica. My siblings and I learned from the best mentor in the world that if we were going to achieve our potential in life perseverance, hard work, and integrity would be the determining factors.

My mom lived by example. She was an audacious entrepreneur using her talents and people skills to create a business and provide for her family. She was relentless in teaching us that there were no limits to what we could achieve and where we could go in life. She had big dreams for her kids. It was not up for discussion that we were all going to earn college degrees, have careers, and be independent. She was a creative, out-of-the-box mentor and coach, disciplined and selfless. She not only considered her own children her responsibility but the village's children as well. I still hear stories 17 years after her passing about the impact she had on those around her, whether in Jamaica or the Naperville, Illinois neighborhood where we raised our children. Grandma, as she was affectionately called by everyone in the neighborhood, was always looking out for the kids.

She was the most self-confident and empowering woman I have ever known. She did not define our future by our limited means. We never thought of ourselves as poor—that was a state of mind she did not buy into. She instilled in us the confidence and determination to use our situation as an advantage and motivation in building a prosperous life. Not only that, she also instilled in us the spirit of sharing, giving back and helping others along the way. To whom much is given, much is expected.

It is no surprise that Mama was my greatest influence in my becoming a career mentor, image coach, trainer, and college professor.

So, why did I want to write this book?

As a serial networker, I meet and form deep relationships with professionals "in career transition"—a nice way of saying unemployed. They are baby boomers bumped from the corporate ladder not yet ready to retire, or new college grads and millennials trying to launch their careers. They are predominantly women with superb resumes, educational qualifications, and work experience. They have the skills any company would dream of for their key talent pool.

But why are they in transition—and some over and over again?

They are demoralized. They take it personally. They are loyal to their professions and companies. They cite their education, experience, and loyalty as reasons they should land good jobs and achieve longevity and fulfillment in their careers. They define their worth by the jobs, titles, and companies where they work. They typically have not imagined or explored a different path to prosperity. They do not understand or know their unique value outside of the confines of Corporate America.

I know their stories, I know them personally. I see them at events. I feel their pain. I was one of them. I console and coach them and share career strategies, pointers, tips, and referrals.

But before I go any further, let me share some of their stories.

Yolanda's Story

When Yolanda arrived on the first day for a mid-level operations director position, she was excited at the prospect of helping to lead a new team. She looked forward to working collaboratively with other departments to transform the reputation of the organization into a customer-centric, world-class organization. She immediately faced a reality check that the priority of leaders was immediate expense control, not employee development. New roles were added to her already overloaded plate—lead outsourcing of a significant part of the operation and do so in an unrealistically short timeframe while keeping the organization running. The company kept piling on new responsibilities, so there was no time to think, strategize, lead, spend time with family, meditate, or exercise. Yolanda wanted to spend time developing and empowering her team to enhance team work and productivity. "There is no time for that," she was told. Yolanda had to put out many fires. She attempted to implement professional and team development as a long-term solution to talent recruitment, retention, and profitability challenges. She was repeatedly rejected. Ultimately, Yolanda resigned.

Susan's Story

A highly credentialed senior executive in a well-known firm, Susan had all the requisite degrees and certifications; having seemed to fit the job description to a "T". Susan was personable, had a great resume, solid references, and came from a bigger company. Things went along well as she led her team in delivering on the company's objectives. She didn't make any waves. Susan, however, got a bit nervous when interactions with the CEO did not go well, but refused to push back. She played it safe. Susan is now unemployed for the third time in four years. She now wonders about her next move and worries about the career traction she might be losing. She has no network to call on because she hasn't consistently nurtured one.

Bonnie's Story

A recently promoted millennial senior executive with a global consumer products company, Bonnie sat on the management committee but was never invited to the meetings. Her male colleague, one level her junior, had been attending the meeting prior to her coming on board, and still attended. She challenged her leader's decision to not invite her to the meetings. Bonnie was told they did not want to upset the flow of the committee meeting, but she should rest assured she was doing a fine job.

Yet and moreover, her leader implied that her peers were not comfortable with her, as Bonnie would be the only female on the committee—awkward! She seemed young and not ready for the dog-eat-dog meeting. After several months of lame excuses, Bonnie ultimately prevailed and took her rightful seat at the table.

What do these women have in common? They represent a large segment of our professional worker population who have been rejected and demoralized even though they were loyal, educated, and experienced professionals. They are caught in a tough economy where the jobs they left don't exist anymore and competition is fierce. They have gone through multiple firings, downsizing and sidelining, and have endured unemployment and underemployment for up to five years. They are continuing to look for jobs similar to ones they previously had with companies like the ones they left.

These women span all generations and careers. They are millennial women starting out in their careers with freshly minted degrees, a mountain of college loans with nowhere to go. They are female professionals at every level of the organization chart in every industry.

They are baby boomers, not yet able to afford retirement or just not ready to retire. They are college students trying to figure out a path forward. I get to know them in the college classes I teach. They are vibrant, healthy and creative, and have a great work ethic.

This book is for these hard-working "Everyday Women" who go to work each day to make a living. They are predominantly millennial and baby boomers. They are also breadwinners or from a two-income household.

Men can learn a lot from this book, too. Apart from the obvious fact that all men have or have had women in their lives—mother, sister, daughter, wife, cousin—men are the primary leaders of these women's careers. They need to understand how to interact with women so that everyone wins. We also know that women are breadwinners, primary caregivers, and chief financial decision makers in households. Consider this:
- "More than 40 percent of mothers are now the sole or primary source of income for the household."
- "Today women make up 47 percent of the labor force."

- "The lesson is clear: if we want to increase the pace of economic growth we should make it easier for more men and women to participate in the labor force."[2]

I am focusing on women because statistics indicates that we are disproportionately disadvantaged. Women typically make only about 70% of a man's salary. We are the "sandwich generation," taking care of several generations of family members (sick or elderly parents and young children). We put ourselves last. We do not own our Power.

I hope to inspire the next generations of women so that my daughter and three grand-daughters own their power and audaciously position themselves to each live an abundant and self-fulfilled life.

Many books have been written about this women's dilemma (*Lean In* by Sheryl Sandberg[3], *The Confidence Code* by Katty Kay and Claire Shipman[4], and *Thrive* by Arianna Huffington[5]). They offer excellent insights and solutions, but most of those popular books come from women of the privileged class who are in a rare place—they have made it. The women I speak to wonder how these women can relate to their plight.

The Audacious Woman, however, takes a bold, optimistic, and practical approach.

This book is meant to inspire and empower women—from millennials to baby boomers—with stories of ordinary women who have successfully made the leap by re-branding and re-inventing themselves and owning their power. What else this book intends is to lay out a step-by-step guide to help women re-imagine success, create a compelling personal brand, radiate a powerful image, blaze a path to prosperity, and live an abundant life.

I am a constant work in progress, thriving through change. I am being stretched out of my comfort zone and learning, loving, and sharing every bit of this journey. I live in gratitude that I have a blessed life. If this book contributes to your audaciously creating a compelling personal brand, owning your power and blazing your trail to prosperity… If it helps to bring you along as one more woman who lives a blessed life, I will consider that I have made a difference.

Audacious Women, we own this challenge and this opportunity to make a difference—in your own life first, and then by helping another woman do the same. It is our time to thrive.

I am doing it! You can too!

Why the Second Edition?

Since the release of the first edition of this book, I have held 50+ eye-opening book-signings, empowerment keynote speeches, and workshops on blazing your own path to prosperity. They were delivered online and on property of libraries, college campuses, chambers of commerce, and in living rooms, with everyday hard-working women and a few men in attendance.

What I discovered is that their overwhelming fear is the same—"We feel trapped in not being able to speak out, afraid of retaliation or losing our jobs."

Simon Sinek in his groundbreaking book says, "… great leaders inspire everyone to take action" by starting with their Why. When my dear friend and collaborator, Peggy, suggested that I update my book and re-release it, I had to think about it—what would my Why be? Upon revisiting the prologue of this book, I found my Why described as "to inspire everyday women and the next generations of women to own their power and audaciously position themselves to live abundant lives."

I further stated, "Men can learn a lot from this book… they are the primary leaders of women's careers. They need to know how to interact with women so that everyone wins." And with that, I immediately felt inspired and compelled to write the words contained in the new chapter, "The Audacity to Disrupt the Status Quo."

So, what can I hope to accomplish by sharing this new content? I need to know that I did everything I could to affect change. Otherwise, how else would I look at my children, granddaughters, grandsons—and all who see me as a mentor and role model—in the face if I did nothing?

It's not a coincidence that I am writing this call to action on the dedicated Martin Luther King weekend. Exactly three years ago I wrote the original "Audacity to Dream" chapter in which I highlighted this civil rights icon as the Ultimate Dreamer who transformed the world.

Synchronicity at Its Best

Earlier this year, my husband and I sat immersed in the message our pastor was delivering at the church we attend. He announced that the theme in his weekly messages for the month would be,

"The Audacity to Dream." My husband and I could hardly contain ourselves!

When I reminded our pastor about the synchronicity of that moment—that this is the same theme as the second chapter of my book—we were both so excited. He and I decided to do workshops and get the message out to our church family and beyond… create a wave!

Aha!

We women and men can boldly co-create a world where all of us can live in harmony and prosperity—where mutual respect is the new norm.

So, Peggy, thanks for sowing the idea. I enthusiastically take the challenge.

And yes, I am moved to seize this moment.

So, let's get to work!

CHAPTER 1 - FROM CAREER TRANSITION TO LIFE TRANSFORMATION

> *"Twenty years from now you will be more disappointed by the things that you didn't do than by the ones you did do, so throw off the bowlines, sail away from the harbor, and catch the trade winds in your sail. Explore, dream, discover."*
> ~ Mark Twain, source unverified

So many of us go through life drifting from one mediocre career to another—always wondering "what if."

What if I tried a new career path that I'm passionate about?

What if I could pursue a path that had a real impact on someone's life or career?

Do you jump out of bed every morning excited about the day ahead? You dream about doing work that you are passionate about—work that will lead you into a prosperous future.

At some point, we wrestle with the decision of whether to take a risk and move our career and lives into uncharted territory. For most of us, our dreams never come true. When we have these dreams, we are quickly jolted back into reality. We have to pay bills, so we continue on the current path because that is what we studied for, or where we invested five, ten, or fifteen years of our lives. Moreover, our social identity is aligned with our employment. Have you ever tried explaining to your family or professional colleagues what you do if it doesn't have a specific label? Good luck!

A recent study, as cited by a Forbes.com staff writer, showed that 52.3% of Americans are unhappy in their jobs.[1] What worried workers most? Job security. Many say they would like to change careers; however, few will take that bold step to discover, take risks, and change the trajectory of their lives until some event jolts them into action. That is exactly what happened to me.

My Transformation Story

It was a beautiful Friday afternoon in August 2010. I had been working from home when my "AHA" moment happened. Put simply, I had another in a series of unfulfilling job experiences and stressful conversations with my then-leader.

Before, when having those experiences, I would shake them off and get back to work. This time, however, was different. I had previously set life objectives and defined workplace parameters that would influence decisions about my life, from that point forward. I did some soul-searching over the weekend about how much longer I would tolerate yet another corporate roller-coaster ride, when I knew in my heart that there was much more I wanted to do to serve others and to be fulfilled.

> *"Leap and the net will appear."*
> ~ Zen proverb

I decided with great trepidation it was time to leap. I heard my mother's voice whispering to me, "Now is the time to do it." At the same time, I had a conversation with my husband, discussing what I was about to do—formally resign and start my own business. My husband and strongest supporter, agreed. He said, "We'll work it out, go for it."

It was scary to walk away from a six-figure salary, especially given the tenuous global economy and dismal job market in South Florida. My life's plan had slotted retirement in only a few years. But I knew in my gut that the moment had arrived to re-invent my career, chart a new course, and claim prosperity. I decided I would no longer transition from one job to the next. I was about to transform my career and my life. And then, I experienced the most liberating feeling of my life.

The Birth of *Ultimate Image Coach*

By the time I arrived at my office the following Monday to formally resign, I had already moved into high gear to initiate plans to launch *Ultimate Image Coach*, a personal branding and image consultancy. The specific goal was to help others manage their careers, re-invent themselves, create a compelling personal brand, radiate a powerful image, and achieve their maximum potential.

I immediately continued the process of building my personal brand. Already known as an avid networker in South Florida, I kicked up my networking activities by several notches, attending two to three events per week. My initial activities included training and coaching unemployed professionals at local unemployment offices and outplacement firms, develop personal branding skills, and polish their professional image in preparation for networking, interviewing, and negotiation.

Driven by Passion, Fueled by Confidence

How did I get the confidence to put myself out there as a personal branding and image consultant?

I had been on the professional image coaching journey years before, as a corporate executive. As a seasoned human resource, customer service, and operations executive, I took it upon myself to develop and coach colleagues and team members on appearance, behavior, and communication, which are the most critical workplace success skills.

My Click Moment

> *"....When you dig deep into the actions of successful people and organizations, you'll find a common theme. A turning point occurs...an unlikely idea surfaces and they take advantage of that serendipity to change their fate."*
> ~ Franz Johannson, The Click Moment[2]

Becoming a Professor of Business and Human Relations is one of the most rewarding adventures of my life. I wish I could say it was part of my grand strategy, but the truth is that it was pure serendipity, or my "Click Moment," as Franz Johansson calls it. A dear friend and neighbor, who I met at our gym purely by accident, asked what I was up to. I told him I had resigned from my corporate job to start my business. He suggested that I should share my corporate and image expertise as an adjunct professor at Palm Beach State College where he is a professor. He thought the students would benefit greatly from some of my real-world experience. He invited me to the campus and introduced me to the credentialing manager. I was immediately credentialed to teach Management, Human Relations, and Customer Relations courses. As it turned out, the college had my transcripts in their system for four years, and the credentialing manager was able to retrieve my information and make an informed decision.

It couldn't have turned out better if I had planned it. That was about four years ago. I now conduct public and corporate training and workshops on behalf of the college and for my business, *Ultimate Image Coach*. The fact that the courses I teach are completely aligned with my brand makes it so special. I have learned more from my students and colleagues than I ever imagined.

This "Click Moment" has changed the trajectory of my brand and business more than any other single planned strategy.

I share this story to demonstrate what this book is about. I made the decision to move from transition to transformation. The decision was radical, the risk was significant, and the life-changing impacts were unpredictable. We were committed for the long haul. I say we because this has been a family journey, it is difficult to do something of this magnitude alone.

Transition to Transformation

Merriam-Webster dictionary says transition is "a change from one thing to the next, either in action or state of being"—as in a job transition, and which is a re-active mindset.

Transformation is "a thorough or dramatic change in form or appearance." This is a proactive, powerful mindset, which says *I own my brand and future success.* Transformation leads you to live your dreams. I like to call it your *"Plan A"* life.

Reality Check.... Most of you will not have the luxury of resigning from your jobs. But you must be prepared for job loss through downsizing, restructuring, layoff, or firing, in its varying euphemisms. You may not technically lose your job, but you might find yourself trapped in a corporate career that is miserable and unfulfilling. You may be living the self-fulfilling prophecy where corporate leaders decide which box you belong in, and you convince yourself that is where you belong. Either way, you have to be prepared to take control of your career and live a prosperous life.

The Worst of Times.... The Best of Times (Are You Living Your Plan A Life?)

If you are doing what you love and living an abundant life, you are living your Plan A life. If you are not doing what you love and find yourself transitioning from job to job, you are living your Plan B life, or someone else's agenda. When I initially shared my transformation story with my business network and friends, the push-back I got in 2010 was that the business climate did not lend itself to taking entrepreneurial risks. They preferred I apply for another less-than-ideal job until the economy settled down.

Note: The Audacious Woman takes a contrarian view—these are the best of times to follow your dream. Moreover, what do you have to lose? You can begin building your path while you look for a new job.

Let's face it. The economy has been scary. Twenty-five percent of jobs lost in the 2008 recession are never coming back. Corporations are playing by new rules, doing more with less staff. I am frequently asked to refer people for job openings, primarily in the Human Resources field. But I noticed a growing, new trend that was becoming permanent: many positions were being consolidated into one.

For example, instead of hiring a Human Relations Analyst or a Compensation Analyst, companies had combined these two roles into one and would add Employee Benefits responsibilities to that position as well. The salary for this combined, new position was often 10–20% lower than it used to be for the previous, individual, streamlined positions.

You do the math—two out of three jobs went away. That was the new reality.

The traditional definition of success has been turned on its head. You need to understand the game, so you can strategize how to play it.... ***or better yet, don't play the game. Instead, create your own path. Build Your Brand! Stand Out! That is what an Audacious Woman does!***

Old Game… Re-active

> *"If you do what you've always done, you'll get what you've always gotten."*
> ~ Tony Robbins

You get your degree, get certified, get hired by the best companies and stay put. If the job does not go well, you quit and find another job. Those days are long gone.

How can you continue to play by the old rules when the corporate hiring and employee development game has changed? Since moving to South Florida, our favorite ice breaker at networking mixers is "where did you relocate from?" The conversation quickly moves to our job status and career opportunities. We are "transplants" from the North who bemoan the fact that we are making fifty percent or less of the salary we made "up North," if we are lucky to be working at all. Most of us are happy to have those jobs, because what could we possibly do instead?

"So, I am in the job market again," seems to be another hot discussion topic at business networking events. What do you do next? You dust off the job search plan you used the last time(s), and reach out to your network for leads and referrals. You update your LinkedIn profile showing in your Headline that you are in transition or available for hire.

New Game: The Hidden Job Market and Other 'Goodies'

Reality Check.... By the time, you pull out your job search plan and notes from the last time you were in transition, and start to blitz LinkedIn with "available for hire" updates and emails, the world will have changed several times over. Opportunities fly by on social networking sites—such as LinkedIn, Twitter, and Facebook—in seconds, not minutes or hours. Relationships are being forged at networking events while you are checking the job postings online. These relationships lead to unprecedented opportunities—for instance, speaking engagements, and volunteer and contract gigs. This is the *Hidden Job Market*. You must be consistently visible and generous with your network. In my strategic networking workshops, the main point I emphasize is that building solid relationships is the most critical part of a successful transformation journey. You will learn more about the reciprocity and benefits of networking later in this book.

The New Game is developing, managing, and leveraging your personal brand. This is the game plan whether you want to become an entrepreneur or make an impact as a corporate employee—a path I will call "intrapreneurship."

It has been reported that since the recession of 2008, companies have adopted a new talent strategy—staff with independent contractors who are not permanent, yet who are full-time professionals, just as they had employed not so very long ago.

Let's position ourselves for this new reality.

As John Canfield says, "Don't worry about failures, worry about the chances you miss when you don't even try."

Change your mindset from "For Hire" to "Brand You"—*a Compelling Personal Brand (Audacious Brand)* uniquely equipped to solve any firm's or client's business challenges.

Re-focus! Change your perspective. Identify your purpose and let that drive you to accomplish your life's dreams. Caution: The journey will be long and winding. You will doubt yourself. You will fail. If you don't, that means you're not pushing the envelope or being audacious enough.

The new game requires you to:
- Discover what makes you unique
- Develop new skills and confidence
- Become the best at whatever you do
- Make your own free agent deal
- Be your self-promoter/PR agent

Here's a tough one for women to swallow—you don't have to be perfect to launch your dream business or land your dream job. I recently asked a group of women entrepreneurs and corporate professionals if they would apply for a position or bid on a piece of business if they were less than 70% qualified to do the work. The resounding answer was "no." Well, what answer do you think you'd get from men? "Hell, yes!" They would hire or subcontract an expert to shore up their deficient areas and move on to the next deal. We can learn a thing or two from men. And then, surpass them!

Since we started the *Image, Personal Branding, and Career Empowerment* movement, I presented over 100 workshops, keynotes, and one-on-one sessions across the U.S. We were overwhelmed by the high interest in what we offered. People of all demographics were seriously stepping up, leaning in to take control of their professional lives, and looking for solutions—both branding and image—to stand out from the crowd. They were looking for inspiration and the step-by-step guide to transformation.

They were looking for a new, practical path forward, but didn't know how or where to start. My daughter, and business partner, and I found that most of our seminar attendees, clients, and networking friends seeking to enhance their brand were baby boomer and millennial women.

Statistics show that baby boomer women are the new power consumer. They want to improve themselves personally and professionally and are hungry for tools, strategies and experiences they can relate to. This trend is great news for my business. The millennial female has more ambition and education than work experience and defines success differently. The boomer woman knows she's getting slowly pushed out of C-suite jobs—corporate level positions—to make room for a younger, cheaper model, and who is not ready for retirement.

As a new entrepreneur, I related to the concerns my baby boomer clients and audiences felt. I shared my experiences, ups, and downs. The message of *Ultimate Image Coach* during the personal branding and image workshops, and keynote presentations resonated in South Florida, Atlanta, Georgia, Washington, D.C., and on social media sites. People asked how I mustered the confidence to take such a bold, entrepreneurial move, and what steps I had followed. When my daughter, Tamara Toussaint—a law school graduate who had previously worked for a law firm—joined our fledgling business a couple years later, we got even more questions about how we were able to pull it off.

What Makes Us Unique? Our Brand

Authenticity. We reflect our brand. We were constantly approached by people who remarked,

"You ladies should be in the personal branding or image business." Or, "You look the part."

Realistic Expectations. We did not sugar coat anything. We laid out the difficult choices and sacrifices we had to make.

Diverse Experience. Tamara is particularly effective with millennial women, who we found were very eager to define success differently, and take control of their futures at a much earlier point in their career.

What made our partnership so effective and impactful is the diverse backgrounds, personality, and demographic differences we brought to the business. I, the corporate veteran, related to the boomer woman and her challenges. Tamara, the younger business woman, is much more in tune with the millennial's view of success and out-of-the-box-nothing-to-lose way of thinking because her career has yet to take off. Innovation, engaging presence, and relatability are her trademarks.

In the rest of the book, we will take you on a transformational journey. This is not about baby or incremental steps. It's about taking risks and boldly branding and re-writing our life *stories.*

You are now in charge of your destiny. Transform your perspective. Unleash your personal brand. Define success on your terms. Create new paths to prosperity and live an extraordinary life. You are in control.

Are you ready to throw off the bowlines and leap into your future?

CHAPTER 2 - THE AUDACITY TO DREAM & IMAGINE PROSPERITY

"Imagination is the workshop where are fashioned all plans created by People. The impulse, desire, is given shape, form and action through the aid of the imaginative faculty of the mind."
~ Napoleon Hill, *Think and Grow Rich*[1]

You are taking the first step of the transformation journey.

What is the future you envision? In your quiet moments of reflection, what do you dream about and how will it change the world or, at least, your world?

How many times have you said to yourself, "If I had the power to change this situation, or if I won the lotto, I would do this or that?" The first step requires you to dream, imagine, and visualize your future.

As I am finalizing this chapter, there are a number of events unfolding across the world that help to demonstrate what the "Imagine Prosperity" step is all about.

First, the Martin Luther King, Jr. holiday, which is a few days away, has inspired me. Dr. King is the greatest, most inspiring dreamer, civil rights leader, and orator on earth. He has made an indelible impact on people across the world. He had a dream that he was able to describe in such eloquent, inspiring, and concrete terms. Decades after his death, his "*I Have a Dream*" speech stands out as the greatest oratorical work and inspiration of all times.

> *"I have a dream that one day right there in Alabama little black boys and little black girls will be able to join hands with little white boys and white girls as sisters and brothers."*
> ~ Martin Luther King, *I Have a Dream*

Do you have a clear picture of what your ideal future or prosperity looks like? Dr. King's dream is very intimidating to emulate, but he inspires us to visualize the future we want and make it happen, regardless of race. This chapter is about the visualizing part of your transformation journey. In the upcoming chapters, you will learn about the steps to create your brand and make your dream a reality.

Another event which happened—and is a bit more relevant to the focus of this book—is Ann Curry, veteran NBC News correspondent, announced her resignation from the network. She was fired from NBC's *The Today Show* in 2012, supposedly for not being able to get along with co-anchor Matt Lauer. She continued, however, to do special projects for NBC. Ann is ultimate class and grace. I have seen some of her specials. She brings cultural awareness and respect to the world leaders whom she interviews. Ann reportedly struck a deal with NBC where she would create content and run her own show distributed on alternative media. In parting, she said, "I want to expand my drive to give voice to the voiceless..."

Ann's experience and audacious act to take control of her career and life is not unique. As the article indicates, "She is following a path others, in similar situations, have blazed."[2] The "others" include Soledad O'Brien of CNN, Meredith Viera, also of NBC, and most notably the now-retired, Barbara Walters, formerly of NBC.

What does prosperity mean to you? Webster Dictionary defines it as "the condition of being successful or thriving; especially: economic well-being." I want to expand on this definition by focusing on well-being, abundance, and happiness.

As a personal branding coach and professor, I come across many young women who are quite open to risk-taking. They are willing to explore entrepreneurial and non-traditional paths to success. Their view is that their careers have not yet taken off—even up to seven years after graduation—so, why not try something completely new?

Kathy's Story

Kathy, a millennial professional with an advanced degree—but little corporate experience—decided to explore different career paths before settling on a career she was passionate about. She took a corporate job in a field she was qualified for with the goal of learning valuable skills, and, in addition, build a career with the company. But, Kathy had a horrible experience. The company had a rigid, old-boys' culture and provided its employees with no formal training. Kathy had no mentors within the company, her boss was a micro-manager, and she received no performance feedback. The culture was such that sexist comments were made to and about female employees. She was ultimately fired, not due to performance, however, but to not fitting in. She struggles to find what's next.

Kathy ultimately explores, and takes the plunge into, an entrepreneurial path and joins a start-up. She finds her passion as a corporate trainer. Only through this plunge into the unknown path, does Kathy realize that she loves the excitement of building a business, interacting with clients and training groups on the topics of professional image and personal branding. She enjoys the constant interaction and also the freedom of managing her schedule. Shortly after working with this start-up and gaining valuable experience in corporate training, Kathy is able to find her dream job with a major corporation doing training. She loves the company's entrepreneurial culture. Kathy is able to maintain her ability to set up her own schedule, work from home, and is provided with an amazing training and professional development program.

Kathy's story is commonplace. I have several millennial clients, mentees, and friends experiencing significant career setbacks and uncertainty. I strongly believe they are struggling to find their career footing a lot more than previous generations of women. The statistics bear that out.

"'Most of these young people have come out of college or graduate school with horrendous student debt into a job market where there are not very many jobs,' Katherine Nordal, executive director for professional practice of the APA, told *NBC Nightly News with Brian Williams*. 'This has put their life plans probably on hiatus; they may be postponing marriage, postponing having a family.'

"The APA survey also revealed that 76 percent of Millennials surveyed say that work is a somewhat or significant stressor, compared to 65 percent of Gen Xers and 62 percent of Boomers."[3]

The job market, career progression, education, and health care continue to be major challenges for even the most educated.

Here is what I imagined. I imagined a work world where everyone had the opportunity to dream, be confident, enjoy a career where they could thrive, and live an abundant life. Everyone would have the opportunity to innovate and contribute to build a successful economy and, in so doing, create a successful and abundant path for themselves.

I was able to help Kathy transform her career, restore her self-confidence and brand herself as a corporate trainer, even though she was turned down two years before as not having the confidence and skills to be taken seriously.

One of my biggest frustrations as a corporate leader was to see how much other corporate leaders wanted from employees with so little nurturing, grooming, and encouragement. I knew our employees were hard working, technically adept folks, but for the most part, they had no mentoring to handle the tricky path of corporate politics. They were petrified of making a mistake or failing.

I loved helping junior associates, colleagues, and clients find their voice and exhibit great people skills—a positive attitude and image, behavior, communication, and likeability. I would spend a bit more time with them than was expected by leaders. I was often asked why I was doing this. The push-back I got from my leaders was that those employees are college graduates—they should come with all the skills necessary to succeed.

Susie's Story

Let's take Susie; a sharp technician, financial analyst, and a genius with systems, technology, and process. She was the undisputed "go-to" person in a department of about 100 employees. Susie was painfully shy and would not speak up in project meetings. She always worked behind the scenes and someone else would present her work, often taking the credit. Her self-esteem and self-confidence were low. Susie had no mentor or any senior person who took an interest in helping her develop the soft skills necessary to thrive and succeed in the corporate world.

When I became her leader, I worked with her on her people skills and self-confidence. I coached her to take speaking roles in meetings and lead projects where she was the expert. At first, she was so nervous about speaking in front of people, her voice would quiver. With positive reinforcement from colleagues and more coaching, Susie made great strides in finding her voice and confidence. She ended up, within a year, being among the most highly rated employees in the 100-person service center. She was sought out by many departments for project participation.

I convinced a few of my leaders and colleagues that investing in employee development strengthens company performance, creates a deep bench of empowered employees, and enhances the overall image of the company as a great place to work.

Here is what I imagined. I imagined a future where everyone from middle school, high school, college to baby boomers and beyond had access to training and coaching on personal branding, professional presence, and human relations. These skills can be learned, and they are critical to personal and professional success.

I realized that helping people develop self-confidence and radiate a powerful image was a deep passion. My colleagues reinforced my self-assurance that I was "born to help people."

I enjoyed a fabulous thirty-plus-year career as a corporate HR and client services executive. I had been rewarded with good compensation, gratifying work, and responsibilities. I was in constant motion doing the corporate jobs, agreed to unreasonable deadlines, exceeded targets, all the while displaying poise and grace under fire during the most stressful situations.

However, I had this itch that there was more to Success and Prosperity than the corporate job.

So, I continued to mentor and coach junior professionals while still employed.

Baby Boomer Women Audaciously Seeking Their 2nd or 3rd Act

Whether they were bounced off the corporate ladder way too early to make room for younger models, severed in the budget cut, or resigned to pursue their passion as I did, my fellow boomer women are on a sprint to explore new paths. They want to improve themselves in every way health-wise, start a new career or business, travel, and have fun. The boomers give new meaning to "60 is the new 40." They are not ready for this thing people call retirement. I can attest that in my hometown of West Palm Beach, Florida, we boomers are responsible for the Zumba tsunami that has taken over the nation! We dance, our body image improves, and so does our self-confidence. We love—and buy—nice clothes and shoes. We believe we can do anything we want. Recent studies show that boomers are the most powerful consumer-spending demographic, controlling 85% of consumer expenditures.[4]

Boomers are forming new business at a fast clip and want to exude a powerful image and be taken seriously. So, yes, I have quite a few boomer clients seeking to re-brand and stand out from the pack. Here's what's so great about boomer women: they have discovered—or re-discovered—their self-confidence; they play by their own rules.

What does success mean to you? What does it look like? If you could throw out society's norms and expectations and re-invent your career path, create a compelling brand, and envision prosperity and abundance, what would you do?

> *"If you don't build your dream, someone else will hire you to help them build theirs."*
> ~ Dhirubhai Ambani, *Against All Odds: A Story Of Courage, Perseverance And Hope*[5]

I challenge you to dream big and think about the activities that energize you and make you stand out from the pack. Go after them with confidence and purpose.

Now, let me be absolutely clear. It's not going to be easy. You will have many doubts and stumbles and failures, but dogged determination will get you there.

You now hold a picture of what your future looks like. Next, how do your passion and strengths play into making that picture a reality and define your purpose? The transformation journey continues.

CHAPTER 3 - FIND YOUR PERSONAL BRAND SWEET SPOT

"Every dream begins with a dreamer. Always remember, you have within you the strength, the patience, and the passion to reach for the stars to change the world."

~ Harriett Tubman

Passion is the Driver

You are a brand! Own it!

In my personal branding workshops and coaching sessions, I usually get blank looks from my career transition clients when I ask them what they are passionate about. Many say, "Who cares what my passion is?" Or "I don't have a passion, I just need a job." If you don't know what you are passionate about, you will continue to transition from one job to another with the same unfulfilling result of living someone else's agenda. I encourage my audience that the best time to explore their passion and begin the transformation journey is while they are in transition.

While sharing a few experiences that led to joy and fulfillment, I notice that my participants' faces light up, they become energized, and the passion stories start pouring out.

> *"What makes you special, what do people you know think about you, what is your passion, ever complimented or rewarded for a talent?"*
>
> ~ Seth Godin, *Purple Cow*[1]

Lindreth's Story, Stiletto Cakes

A delectable work of art is how I describe *Stiletto Cakes*. I first met Lindreth Miller at a weekend women's retreat where I was speaking about personal branding and the power of image. I was immediately taken in by her warm and spiritual personality. Lin shared with me that she was at a cross-roads in deciding between pursuing her passion or continuing her career-journey as a nurse. When she shared with me her passion and burning desire to launch her business as a cake artist/entrepreneur, I just knew her journey and story would be powerful to share.

I kept in touch with Lin and invited her to my firm's *Holiday Pop of Color Networking* reception. She delighted everyone with a generous supply of cupcakes, so artistically decorated and presented, that we were reluctant to disrupt the work of art, but happy we did because they were amazingly delicious. The best part was seeing Lin's personality shine through. She radiated pride, confidence, and joy at her creation. It was clear she was born to be a cake artist!

Lin says, "Baking has always been a soother for my soul! My home was known to have something sweet to share with friends and family. My friends and family always mentioned to me to open a business and sell my cakes and desserts. I never took them seriously; I really thought they were being polite! I've worked in the medical field for twenty-four-plus years as a registered nurse. I found my work-life becoming stressful and affecting my home. I had no idea what I would do. I began to pray and search guidance from people I admire and love. Most importantly, I consulted my better half, who has given me excellent advice and support!"

Lin has followed her passion, discovered her personal brand, and launched *Stiletto Cakes*. She creates the most beautiful cakes for all occasions while she continues her nursing career.

Spend time to discover what makes you feel fulfilled, self-expressed, and let that passion trigger your brand journey and let the world know about it. I find those who are in touch with their passion and strengths, and use them to create their personal brand, are much happier, present a confident image, and are more successful in securing jobs and business opportunities, than higher, technically, skilled people.

Four Keys to Personal Branding

Key #1. Ask yourself, "Who am I?" "What's my story?" Every personal brand journey starts with a compelling story. Go back to your childhood days, if you need to. Ask those close to you to help. What are you known for?

If I asked a hundred of your friends and acquaintances to describe your brand, "Googled" you, or checked you out on social media sites—such as Facebook, LinkedIn, or Twitter—what recurring theme would I uncover?

What makes you unique? Do you love to care for seniors, design cars, or draw pictures? Or did you like to teach school to your fellow five-year-olds? Put together a composite and you will see your passion emerge.

What are you passionate about? What life and career experiences give you a feeling of pure joy? Do you ever feel so fully energized or lost in what you are doing that time gets away from you? You may hear artists or authors describe this feeling that keeps them working and creating into the wee hours of the morning.

Knowing who you are is the most important step. Your personal brand should be clear, consistent, authentic, memorable, meaningful, and personal. Think of a famous brand and describe how they stand out from the pack. Why are they authentic?

Mihaly Csikszentmihalyi—one of the pioneers of the scientific study of happiness—discovered "people find genuine satisfaction during a state of consciousness called 'Flow.' In this state they are completely absorbed in an activity, especially an activity which involves their creative abilities. During this 'optimal experience' they feel 'strong, alert, in effortless control, unselfconscious, and at the peak of their abilities.'"

He says in these moments, "you forget yourself and begin to act effortlessly, with a heightened sense of awareness of the here and now. Athletes often describe this as 'being in the zone.'"[2]

This is what passion will drive you to do and to feel.

I experience "flow" when I am working with teams or working one-on-one with a client mentoring, developing, and executing a personal branding plan; or preparing a client for a presentation or interview. I also get that feeling when conducting training for sales, leadership, or a customer service team on image management skills and customer loyalty skills. I chuckle (smile) when I discuss this step because I sometimes get so caught up in the moment that my one-hour coaching sessions often turn into two or more hours, leaving my husband to ask on a few occasions, "How do you make money doing this?"

Key #2. Ask yourself, "How do my strengths play into my passion?" "What skills and strengths do I bring to the table and what drives me to do what I do?"

Is it your desire to help others succeed? Do you dream of using your social media or organization skills to work on a civil rights or political campaign? Are you driven to use your talent to give voice to and put a positive light on a country or a people who are not usually positively represented in the media?

Diana's Story, Digital Media Specialist, The Real Haiti Entrepreneur

When I met Diana Pierre-Louis, she was digital media manager for the local college where I teach. We immediately developed a professional and personal friendship. As my digital media specialist, I admire her talent, creativity, and warm spirit.

When Diana fell in love with her husband, Endy, she also fell in love with his native country, Haiti. Years after Diana and Endy married, she is now an advocate and philanthropist for Haiti. Through her blog, *The Real Haiti*[3], she educates others about the country through videos, photography, and written experiences. Diana's passion for the island won her an award from Haiti's Minister of Tourism for creating the country's slogan, "Experience It," which is seen and heard throughout the island and nationwide.

In her own words, "I am a multi-level public relations professional with extensive knowledge of social and digital media. My experience involves large in-house marketing, digital media, public relations, media relations, and blogging."

Diana used these skills and strengths to promote her passion for Haiti. What a beautiful story!

Do you feel strongly about playing a key role in empowering women leaders, building the next generation of strong, confident women leaders, and leaving a legacy for your children and grandchildren?

Natalie Madeira Cofield, Walker's Legacy

A millennial that found inspiration at the nexus of business, community, and politics, Natalie Cofield has carved a niche for herself as an entrepreneur, advocate, and speaker on all things business and diversity. Natalie had been inspired by the story of Madame C. J. Walker, the Ultimate Audacious Woman, and formed *Walker's Legacy*, a women-in-business initiative designed to help women walk into their professional passion and purpose.

Natalie invited my daughter, Tamara, to speak at a *Walker's Legacy* event in Washington, D.C., several years ago. Tamara was so impressed by the mission and vision of the movement, and by the energy of Natalie and other members of the team, that she became a strong supporter. Tamara is now a leader of the movement in the Washington, D.C. area.

Madame C.J. Walker says, "I am a woman who came from the cotton fields of the South. From there I was promoted to the washtub. From there I was promoted to the cook kitchen. And from there I promoted myself into the business of manufacturing hair goods and preparations. I have built my own factory on my own ground."[4]

Madame Walker remains a powerful inspiration to women from all walks of life.

Michelle Diffenderfer, Environmental Lawyer, Leader

I met Michelle through a mutual friend who thought she and I certainly needed to connect, and that she would be perfect to profile in my book. Her professional accolades and success are very impressive, but more importantly, Michelle cares about empowering women and young girls. A mother of two young daughters, she serves as a role model for women finding their voice and achieving their potential in a male-dominated world. She teaches by example the soft power traits women leaders should embrace.

Michelle's LinkedIn profile reads:

> *Michelle is President of the law firm of Lewis, Longman & Walker, P.A. and holds an AV Preeminent Rating by Martindale-Hubbell. Her practice focuses on environmental, water, natural resources, and land use law, specifically, permitting and enforcement.*
>
> *Michelle is in Leadership Florida's XXXIII Class, serves on the board of the Southeast Florida Coral Reef Initiative Board, the board of Girls II Women, and serves pro bono as General Counsel of Northwood GREENlife. Michelle remains an active member of the American Bar Association's Section of Environment, Energy and Resources participating in various Committees.*[5]

I want to dispel the myth that personal branding is just for entrepreneurs, entertainers, or people with a major platform. It is just as important to create a powerful brand or name for yourself in a corporate setting or while in college.

As a corporate executive, the candidates I gravitated to—whether hiring new people or dealing with succession planning—were not the most technically adept, but those who had a point of view, who stood out from the pack with high-energy, creativity and the confidence to communicate what they believed in. Companies do not look for carbon copies, they seek people who challenge the status quo, who stretch themselves and, hence, the company to explore new paths and grow businesses.

Key #3. Who is your target audience? Who are you going to serve?

Clarity around your target audience is absolutely essential. Are you focusing on entrepreneur and small business clients involved in manufacturing or commercial construction? Or, will you be serving colleges, conference planners or baby boomer women re-entering the job market? What are their needs? Have you done your market research? Who are your competitors? If you don't know who you are serving and what their needs are, how can you solve their problems?

How you position your brand truly is where the rubber meets the road. For this reason, I devote chapter 4 entirely to **Key #4**, sharing tips and strategies to differentiate your brand and stand out.

CHAPTER 4 - DIFFERENTIATE AND DISRUPT

"...J.K. Rowling and Oprah Winfrey didn't become a couple of the wealthiest people on earth by trading physical labor for a salary; they used creativity and harnessed the power of leverage brilliantly."
~ Randy Gage, *Risky is the New Safe*[1]

A Category of One, or Uniquely You

Imagine a room full of entrepreneurs and other business people at a networking event where you do the customary 30-second introduction—AKA the elevator pitch. At the end of it, you ask yourself how was person "A" different from "B" or "C"? What does each one really do? Everybody sounded like everyone else. They did not stand out from each other.

I have had clients who asked, "Why am I not getting any traction at these business networking events? I show up, I deliver my elevator pitch, pass around business cards, and set up appointments, but nothing happens." The usual issue is the failure to clearly communicate a compelling personal brand, and value to the potential customer.

As Seth Godin says, you should aim to be the Purple Cow! Stand out!

Clarity and Consistency is Key

I get wary of entrepreneurs who show up at networking events and introduce a whole new business every few months. One month they are selling the new fountain of youth, the next month they are selling financial planning or insurance.

To be taken seriously, you have to find your niche and be authentic and consistent.

To clarify, I am not suggesting that you will be able to position your brand completely right on the first try. On the contrary, as I share below, you will stumble, redo, evolve, and refine it. You will have a higher degree of success and fulfillment when you stay true to what brought you on this journey in the first place.

There is no one recipe for developing your brand and positioning your particular brand, because that would defeat the nature of personal branding. Every brand is unique.

In this chapter I share some tips to help you position your brand, so it resonates with your target market.

The Evolution of My Brand

When I first launched *Ultimate Image Coach*, I was focused on helping folks in career transition—those who were unemployed—re-brand, restore their self-confidence, and launch new careers. I soon realized that my original focus would not be a viable long-term business strategy because most unemployed people could not afford my fees. So, I evolved my brand to focus on businesses and universities, helping them to understand the value of employees personally branding themselves, and exude a polished image and leadership presence. I then added customer relations and soft skills training as a natural evolution of my original brand promise. So, even though I evolved, the core of my business was still personal branding and image.

My son, Gabriel, who has a business development mindset, helped me brainstorm how I could evolve and grow my business and serve a real need in corporate America. He gave me ideas on how to target my ideal client base.

I call him my "out-of-the-box" ideas coach. Today, my corporate clients make up over 90% of my business.

Where the Trail Gets Bumpy and Challenging

Let me share lessons learned, in the form of expectations, and slay a few myths as we embark on this journey together.

Expectation #1. Guts (Risk-taking)

> *"When you take risks you learn that there will be times when you succeed and there will be times when you fail, and both are equally important."*
> ~ Ellen DeGeneres, *Seriously…I'm Kidding*[2]

It takes guts (audacity) to stand in front of an audience of your entrepreneurial peers or a corporate business leader and put yourself out there as an expert in whatever field you choose. This is a critical part of the branding journey. It is not always a comfortable process. Branding takes a lot of introspection; it takes digging deep into your emotional and cultural values and figuring out how you are going to make this venture work. The question that haunts us all—*What if I fail?* Guess what? You will fail.

The hardest part for most women, especially highly educated and successful women, is accepting that you will fail. Some of the most successful entrepreneurs failed multiple times. What if you don't get it right the first time? Tweak your brand, stay abreast of trends, and evolve your business. Take it from me. The bumps in the road will make you stronger. If you don't fail, that means you are not stretching yourself enough.

I often look to Randy Gage's book *Risky is the New Safe*, for a kick in the shin. Several times I waivered and got cold feet about my decision to go it alone. Do I leave a corporate career with benefits, a steady paycheck—security? Or do I stay, limp along, and defer my dream?

Well, Randy got my attention when he said, "If you are willing to take risks and become a contrarian…there are…and will continue to be extraordinary opportunities for wealth and prosperity."

Expectation #2. A Marathon… Not a Sprint

I have been asked how long it tak es to create your personal brand. Can it be completed in an afternoon at a workshop? The short answer is no. A complete answer depends on a few things. If you are starting from scratch in the discovery phase, the most you can hope for is a rough first draft.

You may remember, in the case of Lindreth Miller, founder of *Stiletto Cakes*, it was so clear what her passion was. She exuded it in every way, as described in her powerful story shared in chapter 3. Lindreth had already done the hard part, which was discovering and exploring her passion.

Developing and positioning your personal brand is not a sprint, but a marathon. It is a journey that is constantly evolving. If you have ever trained for a marathon or any endurance event, you know it requires strong will, resilience, and perseverance. I trained for my first half-marathon when I was over fifty years old. I walked for the American Stroke Association in my mom's memory. I will never forget that experience. It was a combination of pain and exhilaration at the same time.

In a recent speech, I shared with my Chamber Women-In-Business friends that I lost two toenails while training for the first half-marathon. Sure, I thought of quitting. First, it was painful, and second, the nails were going to take up to eight months to grow back. Living in South Florida, where we wear sandals all the time, my feet would not be a pretty sight. My doctor encouraged me, however, saying it was par for the course for marathon trainers, so I decided to bear it, change my walking gear, keep my eye on my goal, and get back on track. I completed the training and the half-marathon, and did two more after that one. The bumps and bruises taught me lessons that helped to navigate the rough and uneven entrepreneurial path.

Myth #1 Personal Branding is Not Necessary to Achieve Success and Prosperity

Here is the hard truth. Either you decide to take control and build your brand or someone else will brand you. In reality, you are already perceived as a brand. Which version would you prefer? Yours or theirs?

For example:

Brand You, through Your Corporation: knowledgeable, subject matter expert, highly regarded, customer-focused project leader.

Brand You, through Their Corporation: competent, knows the products, lacks leadership presence, not presentable to clients.

What do you want to be known for? And how will you position your brand to achieve your objective?

Myth #2 Branding is Only for Entrepreneurs

Before we move on, let me clarify that the tips we share in *The Audacious Woman* are not just for those choosing to explore the entrepreneurial path. If you decide to stay on the corporate track, this is for you, too. You will need to find a company whose brand, or culture, is compatible with yours. You will need creative space to brand yourself and stand out from your competitors in job interviews and on the job.

I recently hosted a webinar with HR folks in transition called "Maximize Your Next Interview with a Compelling HR Brand." Personal branding is even more critical in the HR world because the perception is that HR jobs are shrinking as companies struggle to find the real bottom-line benefit of HR services. I challenged the attendees to throw out the HR job script and mindset. Think like a CEO. What are the most gnawing business issues that keep CEOs up at night? Also, what, in your estimation, are problems CEOs might be faced with which they don't even know? Then channel all of your energies and branding into resolving those issues and make sure you publicize it.

The irony of personal branding is that you can sometimes have a bigger impact on a corporation from outside versus from within the corporate structure.

How to Position Your Brand

Now that we've addressed the expectations and myths, let's focus on the process of positioning your brand.

As Dan Schawbel says, you must leverage your brand "across platforms with a consistent message and image to achieve a specific goal. In this way, individuals can enhance their recognition as experts….establish reputation and credibility, advance their careers, and build self-confidence."[3]

Let's get to work.

How do you stand out? How do others perceive you?

You want to begin by building a profile in people's minds of the brand you want to become. You want to be top of mind among your networking peers and on social networking sites. Here is how it works. If someone is looking for a graphic artist, and you are a graphic artist, your name should be the one that comes to mind at networking events or on social networking sites. The best scenario is to get a strong endorsement from your network. That is gold.

Branding Toolkit Basics

1. **Create a compelling brand offering and message.**

   As highlighted in chapter 3, create a compelling brand offering or promise, and accurately position your brand with your target market. Once you make these two decisions, the rest of the plan flows. This step should be done in a thoughtful and analytical manner.

2. Decide on your target audience.

You should perform market research to discover all you can about your target market. What needs are they known to have? How does your offering solve their problems? Who else is doing the same thing? How do you differentiate and stand out?

3. Create your website.

If you haven't already done so, buy the following two domain names right away: your name, and the name of your business. You would be surprised that the names you thought might be unique to you are already taken. Your website will become the home or anchor for your brand. Get a professional to help you build your site.

4. Level the playing field with social networking tools for the entrepreneur.

"Developing your brand is key to monetizing your passion on line."
~ GaryVaynerchuk, *Crush It*[4]

Social networking is a revolutionary personal branding tool. You can, with a compelling brand and strong marketing message, build a reputation online, create a following, and build your business in a very short time. I am not a social networking expert, but I know enough to share that it is a critical tool to brand yourself and stand out from your competition.

I use LinkedIn, Twitter, Facebook, and YouTube to reach my target market. If you are not comfortable with social networking, get comfortable or hire an intern or social media assistant. Let your target market drive your decision on which sites you use. Caution: Keep up with trends and check that your online brand represents you.

5. Join professional and community organizations.

It is essential to become known in your business community. Join the organizations that will help you promote your brand. If you are targeting the business community, join your local chamber and other business organizations where you are most likely to meet your target market. Diversify your organization affiliation. If you are a customer service professional, join an operations or engineering professionals networking group. Remember, it's all about your target market and getting as many diverse decision-makers knowing about your brand.

6. Volunteer.

Let's face it, most new entrepreneurs do not have a lot of disposable income. We have to manage our cash. A good way to build your visibility is to volunteer at local business events. Volunteer to be a greeter at a huge business breakfast hosted by the local chamber. Arrive early, greet people, introduce yourself, exchange business cards, and follow up. It works. I won a nice training assignment at such an event while serving as a volunteer host.

You will need to give your time, talent, and product to get your business off the ground. In return, you should be building skills that are critical to your brand. For example, if you lack in leadership skills and you consider those skills critical for enhancing your brand, volunteer for a leadership position on a business or non-profit board. Once you are a known brand, make sure you manage how much of your time you give away.

Differentiate and Disrupt

Add the Sizzle

The steps I share above are what everyone is doing and is expected to do. But how do you really get the attention of your target market? How do you add the sizzle so you are getting the attention and monetizing your brand?

Let me be as upfront as I can be; the opportunities are not going to jump out at you. In fact, it is going to take a lot of creativity and focused effort. You have to stay current on what challenges businesses face and see how you can bring a unique angle to solve those challenges. What strikes me at networking events is how many people introduce their business in bland terms that do not address what is in it for the prospective customer or how it solves their problems.

Become a Category of One… Your Niche

We have thousands of career and image coaches on LinkedIn and hundreds in South Florida. I wanted to distinguish myself from the crowd. The following quote bolstered my view that the niche I was carving out was the right one.

> *"Research carried out by the Carnegie Institute of Technology shows that 85 percent of your financial success is due to skills in 'human engineering,' your personality and ability to communicate, negotiate, and lead. Shockingly, only 15 percent is due to technical knowledge."*
> ~ Forbes, *Intelligence is Overrated* [5]

I had found a compelling way to distinguish my brand from everyone else's by focusing on professional presence, human relations, communications, and personal branding, in addition to training individuals on traditional workplace skills.

Empowered by this new-found niche, I set out to volunteer conducting workshops for the local unemployment office and outplacement companies, helping unemployed professionals re-invent their careers, polish their image, and prepare for interviews.

I recommend that you keep your strategy and tactics simple and manageable. It's easy to become overwhelmed. You cannot be all things to all people. That is a surefire way to dilute your brand.

Listen to Your Clients

A few months later, I added a new dimension to my personal branding and image training by incorporating customer service excellence to the mix. When you think about it, the combination makes perfect sense. I got the idea from listening to my clients and they love the combination. I now train managers, sales, and customer service teams.

After four years of evolving and fine-tuning my brand, I now focus on these areas:
- Corporate Training – Image Management, Customer and Human Relations
- Workshops and Keynote Speeches – Unleash Your Personal Brand, Blaze Your Own Path to Prosperity
- Professional Image and Fashion Shows
- Individual Career and Image Coaching

Get on LinkedIn

With over 300 million professionals online, LinkedIn is a personal branding gift. Whether you are a corporate professional transitioning to entrepreneurship, a jobseeker or a recent college graduate, LinkedIn is critical to building your brand. According to LinkedIn's Press Center, more than 2.6 million companies have LinkedIn company pages. A robust LinkedIn profile will have you rising to the top of Google searches.

You don't have to be a celebrity or have your own public relations staff. Having a robust LinkedIn profile and a game plan to engage the public and your target audience with daily updates—share, like, post, invite—gives you a ton of exposure, which exposes your brand and builds your credibility as an expert.

Create Theme Days

In addition to posting my blog on LinkedIn, which feeds to Twitter and Facebook, I wanted to engage my target market in a different way. I designated themes for each day of the week and created an image with key words to represent those concepts. I use the visual as a header to a short write-up, and then create a link to my website. This conveys my brand message in a crisp and eye-catching manner, in which drives traffic to my website. To see how the themed days look, visit https://www.linkedin.com/in/pamelatoussaint.

Add a Facebook Page

Janet Silvera was recently named Jamaica's 2014 "Print News Journalist Of The Year," bringing to 15, the number of awards Silvera has won in recent years. She has spent the last 20 years with *The Gleaner*, mainly as coordinator of the island's sole tourism-trade publication, *Hospitality Jamaica*.

My sister, Sandra, introduced me to Janet over the phone. She thought Janet would be a perfect person to profile as an audacious woman. Janet and I have become Facebook friends. She uses Facebook very effectively to brand herself, and Jamaica as a fun and exciting place. Whether sharing personal stories or updates on "goings-on" or breaking news in Jamaica, Janet gets my attention. She is engaging. She keeps up a conversation with her Facebook tribe. I look forward to Janet's Facebook posts. She is an image consultant's dream! She always looks stylish and confident! She makes me want to jump on a plane and join her at the party or event!

It's all about Videos

Personal Branding experts say that this is the year of the videos. Are you adding a video clip to your blog, LinkedIn, or website? Just think about it. We have these smartphones, which are excellent cameras, and the videos they produce are easy to upload to your social networking sites, such as YouTube. I will be doing much more with videos for these very reasons.

Launch Your Own TV or Radio Show

Why not? In a recent discussion with women entrepreneurs, I asked them how they were planning to differentiate their brand. I was delighted to hear one of them say she is starting her own radio show. How awesome!

The key to executing and monetizing your brand is to develop a plan, do your homework, know what you don't know, learn and surround yourself with people who are trustworthy and will enhance your brand.

The branding journey is an evolving and learning experience. I am a brand in progress. I am trying out new approaches all the time to maximize my visibility and reputation.

As Alvin Toffler says, "The illiterate of the 21st century will not be those who cannot read and write, but those who cannot learn, unlearn, and relearn."

CHAPTER 5 - RADIATE A POWERFUL IMAGE

"If you want to know what your single most powerful competitive edge is, just look in the mirror. That's right, it's you."
~ Jeb Blount, *People Buy You*[1]

Three Seconds!

That's how long it takes to make a first impression that can have a lasting impact on your business and social life.

Do you ever wonder how one woman can walk into a room and heads turn? Everyone gravitates to her. She exudes an engaging, warm presence that is irresistible. She is the magnet which draws attention to her. She creates a positive, memorable impression. Contrast this with another woman who walks into the same room and is so uncomfortable and self-conscious that she hangs around at the farthest end of the room, and does not make eye contact or attempt to meet anyone.

This is the power of first impressions. We can all think of people who fall into both camps.

Yet, if they fall into the latter category of being uncomfortable or self-conscious, they may be given the benefit of the doubt from that first critical encounter. However, be aware it is said that it takes up to ten interactions to reverse a negative first impression.

The Double Standard

There is absolutely no doubt that we women are judged by our appearance, actions, and communications more than men. From the moment we enter a room, we are examined from head to toe—our attire, hair, eye contact, smile, and communication style. You may dismiss this as superficial, but it is real, and impacts your ability to be taken seriously in business and social settings.

Let's take First Lady Michelle Obama, for instance. Who among us was not guilty of anticipating what her outfit would be for a White House gala, inaugural, or state visit? Mrs. Obama's impressive Harvard Law degree, her stint as a hospital executive, and her leadership on issues of national and global importance, comparatively, seem to take a back seat, even today.

In over three decades as a corporate HR executive, personal branding coach, professor, and speaker, I have experienced the power of image as a key determinant of one's success in business and life. The good news is that a person's image can be enhanced and transformed to create a compelling personal brand, and radiate a powerful image consistent with that brand.

Does Your Image Reflect Your Brand?

One of the key reasons entrepreneurs fail is the inability to communicate—both verbally and non-verbally—a crisp, compelling brand. I believe this also applies to career professionals. In other words, if there is a mismatch between what you are claiming as your brand and the one you exhibit through your image—such as appearance, behavior, and communication—your target audience will believe what they can readily see, what you display.

Let's break this down.

Appearance

As an entrepreneur or any business person, you are always in the public eye and under scrutiny. Since women are judged much more than men by the image standard, let's use it to our advantage. The following tips will help you to exude the appropriate image to create the impression you desire.

> *"Wardrobe is critical…you feel and move differently in different kinds of clothes."*
> ~ Harrison Ford, source unknown

Attire choice. Neatness says a lot about your personality. It speaks to your self-esteem, attention to detail, and how you manage yourself and your business.

Color choice. Every color has a message. Use the palette of color choices to your advantage to convey your brand and desired message. For *Ultimate Image Coach*, the brand colors are green and purple (used on a website, business cards, etc.). Green is the color of money, wealth and prestige; and purple is the color of high quality and superior service.

Fit and Style. For the most part, ladies have put away the suits. The business landscape has shifted to one of being less formal. Simply watch female television anchors and guests to see how they are decked out in tailored and colorful dresses, exhibiting a new-found confidence and pride in their femininity. Proper fit, style, and color still apply, however.

How often have you purchased ready-to-wear outfits only to find they seldom fit properly; or the sleeve of a jacket was a half-inch off; or the buttons on the front of the blouse might not be placed in a flattering position, which could result in embarrassing consequences?

You might not be aware of your wardrobe faux-pas, but others will, and that is all they will be focusing on. You could have an irreversible blind spot which could ruin your message. On the flip side, you might be aware of the imperfections in your attire, and become totally distracted by calling attention to it. Your confidence would be impaired.

To not only avoid these distractions, but to ensure your image is spot on, I suggest you secure the services of a seamstress or tailor. A tailored black dress, nicely accessorized with your favorite pumps and a pop of color and jewelry, is always chic, and it hides a lot of sins.

If you are going to be on television, just know that the camera makes you look fifteen to twenty pounds heavier. On the plus side, a warm smile and great posture make you look ten pounds lighter and ten years younger.

Develop Your Signature Style

Be prepared to make a statement. I have found handbags, broaches, a piece of jewelry from a favorite destination, or a scarf are great statement pieces, and make wonderful "ice-breakers" at networking events. My signature piece is a broach. Each one has a story.

Poise and Polish

Your posture, how you walk, and the way you carry yourself speak volumes about your image. Invariably, at business and social events, networking colleagues will comment on how "on-point" and polished my daughter, Tamara, and I look. They ask how we pull it together each time. When I share with folks what I do, they usually say, "You are such a great representation of your brand," or "I totally see you doing that." Well, that's the whole point. Your brand and image are inseparable, and on display every time you interact in person or online. It is the authenticity factor. The scenario I just described represents the way my daughter and I get most of our business, by being poised and polished.

Behavior

Forbes reported that the "Top 3 skills companies hire for are professionalism, high energy, and self-confidence."[2] I couldn't agree more.

Every semester when I meet new students, I can project which ones are going to be successful in my course, no matter what I am teaching at that point. It is not the ones who have the best qualifications or most impressive introduction. But it is the students who conduct themselves in a polished and engaged manner. It is the way they carry themselves. They lean forward and connect. They exhibit an attitude of learning readiness.

Social skills and behavior are key differentiators in one's perception of your brand. Daniel Coleman, the father of Emotional Intelligence (EI), tells us that EI is a much more important determinant of business and personal success than the traditional Intelligence Quotient (IQ) metric.[3]

He breaks it down as follows:
- Self-Awareness: how we come off to other people
- Self-Management: grace under fire
- Social Awareness: how we handle corporate politics

- Relationship Management: communicate effectively and build interpersonal relationships

Often, in personal branding training sessions, college classes, and at networking events, I tell my audience that, in my four-decade career, I have only applied for one job. The rest came as a result of building lasting, reciprocal relationships. I am a serial networker and have been fortunate to prosper in the toughest of economic times. I was not the most technical at any job. I am confident that I have been successful because of my ability to connect with people and form enduring relationships.

It's about being likable and authentic. People do business with people they know, like, and trust. Make sure you are taking every opportunity to be very kind to your customers. Know what makes them happy and deliver.

Communication

Albert Mehrabian is often quoted as saying that the emotional meaning of a message is communicated by:
- Your words, 7%
- Your tone of voice, 38%
- Your body language, 55%[4]

Everything we addressed above in appearance and behavior contributes to the 55%, and why the emphasis is put there.

Tone of voice and the words make up a critical component of overall communication. Women, in particular, must project a positive and powerful tone of voice. This is an area where practice makes perfect and we have the tools (smartphones, tablets) to make ourselves shine. In working with clients, I video-tape their speech practice sessions and play those back to them as part of the feedback. I can't tell you how surprised and disappointed most women are at the sound of their voice and the nervous habits they display. A common problem is the voice rising at the end of a sentence in a questioning fashion. This indicates a lack of self-confidence.

The World is a Stage

We are all actors. So, borrowing from their playbook will help those of us who speak, present, and network for a living. Actors practice getting into character; they rehearse. Here's what I do and coach my clients to do. Practice at home—in front of the mirror—entering a networking event and introducing ourselves. Rehearse in front of the mirror, or a willing family member, or friend, your presentation to a prospect or an audience. A dress rehearsal is essential.

One of the gifts we give to our workshop attendees is a mirror inscribed with the words: ***First Impression$ Matter! We Polish... You Shine!*** When you look in the mirror, your natural reaction is to straighten up and SMILE. Chances are, if you like what you see in the mirror, others will, too. People love these mirrors.

The Audacious Woman's Power Image

Remember that the Audacious Woman doesn't just go for what everyone else is doing. Your goal is to exude leadership presence, stand out, and step up to the front of the line.

In a recent ground-breaking report, *The Center for Talent Innovation* shared some insights into what top global CEOs and business professionals thought were the main issues keeping women from achieving a significant and sustained breakthrough into executive leadership roles:

> *"Looking and acting like a leader depends on getting three things right, a trio we*

refer to as Appearance, Communication, and Gravitas. Individuals who nail each of these elements exude true executive presence." [5]

The study went on to say that women—who seriously lacked these skills and, short of a focused effort to build such skills—would not attain "C-suite" positions in corporate America in significant numbers.

In my estimation, gravitas is the trait most lacking in women. Listed below are attributes pertaining to the poise and dignity of such conduct:
- Command the room
- Decisiveness
- Grace under fire
- Succinct/Convincing

On a recent MSNBC talk show, the editor of *Harper's Bazaar* asserted that women needed to adopt these power moves to bolster their image and be taken seriously. She said women should:
- Always introduce themselves using their first and last name
- Adopt a more open stance
- Accept a compliment in two words, "Thank you!"
- Try out a uniform (or signature style, like a broach)

- Don't accept the first offer
- Order with confidence[6]

Exuding true professional presence and power takes focused work. It requires a combination of coaching, rehearsal, homework, trial and error, and a willingness to make fundamental changes.

You are The Package

> *"The Power Persona is a combination of feminine rapport, masculine strength, and savvy know how… The Power Persona is a trifecta of style, substance, and self-esteem:*
>
> *Signature Style – an engaging presence*
>
> *Synchronized message – relevant and purposeful*
>
> *Self-assured manner – ready to handle anything"*
> ~ Christine Jahnke, *The Well-Spoken Woman*[7]

CHAPTER 6 -
STAND UP! SPEAK UP! POWER UP!

"The Economist magazine recently called female economic empowerment (is) the most profound social change of our times."
~ Katty Kay and Clair Shipman, *The Confidence Code*[1]

Wired For Leadership

"Warren Buffet thinks that women are a major reason why America will do so well, as he stated in a recent essay on women in leadership. Aside from encouraging women to feel more confident in themselves, his bigger plea is to men... The closer that America comes to fully employing the talents of all its citizens, the greater its output of goods and services will be..."[2]

Mr. Buffet goes on to say that women's Emotional Intelligence skills make them more effective leaders than men. Studies show that companies with women leaders are more profitable, have a higher morale, and are more focused on developing and nurturing employees and customers.

The CEO of The Container Store, Kip Tindell, couldn't agree more. He asserts that women make the best executives. Tindell said, "'Intellectual intelligence is really important, but what's more important in a leader is high emotional intelligence. That's why I think women make better executives than men...' About 70% of the top leadership positions at his company are held by women." Tindell also mentioned women are calm and have self-awareness.[3]

But the above example is not the norm in the world of business. Women comprise less than 5% of CEOs in Fortune 500 companies and less than 3% of advertising companies' creative directors.[4]

The Demographic and Economic Power of Women

The facts about women are phenomenal. As of this writing, the female gender in the United States represents the following statistics:
- 50.7% of the U.S. population

- Influence or and buy 80% of all products
- Buy 50% of all electronics purchased
- Spend $5.5–$15 trillion per year in the U.S.

Women also make up 55% of the online population, where 44% of those who use social media as the new word of mouth, gather information, share family updates, enhance skills, send email, and shop. Eighty-eight percent of these women say the Internet simplifies their lives.[5]

Baby Boomer Woman: The Ultimate Power Consumer

Baby-boomer women, those born between 1946 and 1964, represent a portion of the buying public no marketer can afford to ignore. Boomer women are the largest and most powerful demographic, numbering 78 million, or one-third of the U.S. population. They control 70% of U.S. disposable income and spend $2–3 trillion per year.

What do boomer women spend their money on? They seek convenience and service and want it now. They want empathy, advice, education, and self-improvement.

In spite of our economic power, women on the whole make only 70 cents for every dollar a man makes. It's even worse for those women with different ethnic backgrounds.[6]

Why the Leadership Gap?

Our lack of self-confidence gets in the way. The self-talk goes something like this: "I am not experienced enough or I need a few more punches on my corporate ticket before I can do that job." I agree with Sheryl Sandburg who makes this point in her book, *Lean In*.[7] It is true. As a business professor, I can say, without a doubt, that women are typically better students. They study hard, are conscientious, and exceed expectations academically.

However, when it comes to leading a team effort, or delivering the team presentation, the male students step right up while female students lag behind. Most female students are comfortable managing the project plan and preparing the presentation, but will gladly defer to the male students to present. In my own network, we have many overqualified women waiting for the next employer to tap them on the shoulder.

Let's not wait for perfection or someone to validate us. Take control. But I know this bold approach runs counter to our modus operandi. I take every opportunity in the classroom to coach female students to turn around that mindset and step up to the head of the class and lead team projects. In my network, we have many overqualified women waiting for the next employer to tap them on the shoulder.

We are not leveraging our economic power and talents because, as *The Confidence Code* book suggests, "women don't see, can't even envision, what is possible."

Something is wrong with this picture. If, as powerful purchasing influencers we hesitate—or wait—for the status quo to change in our favor, we will be left running businesses from behind, while our male counterparts will have moved on to the next big deal.

The obvious questions jump out: If we are spending this much money, who reaps the benefits? Why aren't we flipping it around and selling services and products to this important demographic—ourselves? We have ready-market data. We know what women want. And yes, we influence over 80% of the buying decisions.

No matter if we are in the boardroom of a Fortune 500 corporation or law firm, a small entrepreneur, or non-profit, we carry huge sway in the economic success of businesses and families. We are the spenders-in-chief. We must now step out of our comfort zone and take the reins of leadership, unleash our power, and not shy away from solving big problems, even if we feel some discomfort along the way. We have to begin building a legacy of leadership so that future generations of women can envision what is possible.

We have to…

Stand up! Speak out! Power up!

Exercise that risk muscle! Think Big! Act! Below are a few suggestions that may trigger even more ideas and action.

1. **Adopt the Male Swagger.**

   Men display that easy confidence which says, "I don't have to go through all of those hoops to be validated." They take a direct, self-confident path to success—all along negotiating their way up the ladder. Women, this has to be the model we embrace! Don't get me wrong. I am not suggesting we act like men. I am suggesting we use our

Unique Female Power Brand to change our mindset, take a seat at the head of the table, and change the world!

2. **Become a Chief Culture Officer or Consultant.**

Women feel disenfranchised and are dropping out of the workforce because they feel disrespected and find the workplace hostile. A White House study reported, "56% of women drop out of computer science professions mid-career—double the rate of men—in some cases because they experience sexist and demeaning workplaces. Specifically, nearly 40% of women who quit science, engineering and technology jobs cite a 'hostile macho culture' as their primary reason for leaving."[8]

The irony here is that a great deal of emphasis is being placed on getting women and girls into Science, Technology Engineering and Mathematics (STEM) education, and fast track their progress into the fields of engineering and technology.

The type of business I am proposing is a confidence-coaching endeavor or a cultural-change consultancy to help company leaders build cultures supportive of the new workplace. It is critical that men are trained, too. I want my granddaughters to grow up in a world where there are no gender-based limitations on their dreams. I see a concrete opportunity to help shape these young women's self-esteem while we educate them on the STEM disciplines.

3. Build Confidence and Entrepreneurship Skills.

We need to start mentoring young girls to be confident and foster the entrepreneurial spirit.

I saw a 15-year-old girl on the television show, *Shark Tank*, stating her case to gain funding for her entrepreneurial venture. She was clear and confident in her presentation to the Shark panel about why they needed to fund her business at the ownership percentage she was proposing. The Sharks pushed back as hard as they could, but she stuck to her guns. She negotiated and was very strong. She exemplified all the qualities we need in our next generation of entrepreneurs...and in the current generation as well.

Encourage women, especially as young

adults, to start businesses. There is an untapped wealth of entrepreneurial opportunities. Women need the confidence, know-how, and access to resources and funding. I would like to see women's groups take on this role in a big way. I commend the *Walker's Legacy* group, introduced to you in chapter 4, for their work on women's entrepreneurship empowerment.

4. Drive Policy Changes.

Work Life Balance Is A Boost To The Bottom-Line.

"'Gallup Poll finds that having access to flexible work arrangements was highly correlated with greater worker engagement and higher well-being.' These policies help businesses attract and retain client, contributing to a business's bottom line.

"One study tracked the announcements of new work-life balance policies by Fortune 500 companies and found firms' stock prices rose 0.36 percent on the days following such announcements, suggesting investors believe these policies to be profitable investments."

~ Nine Facts about American Families and Work, Council of Economic Advisors[9]

What other policy changes could be implemented that would slowly shape a new landscape of the corporate world? One example might be the current bill being submitted to Congress on paid maternity leave.

5. Gain Access to Education Programs.

Join college faculties. As an adjunct professor, I am on the front line of the struggle to help students succeed, but perhaps my biggest challenge is to help female students find their voice and own their power. Addressing the female confidence and image gap should start in grade school. By the time girls reach college, it is much harder to breach these rifts. They need us to balance out the images they consume on television and in the press. It is by this process that we change lives, attitudes, and perceptions of both girls and boys. Include confidence coaching and mentoring at a very early age for girls and boys as young as kindergarteners.

What is the number one topic young career parents talk about all the time? It is the lack of quality and affordable day care. How can we build more quality day and after school programs, provide workplace training either in the local colleges, or develop our own alternate training programs? It's up to us women to drive the sea change needed.

6. Develop and Support Women's Businesses.

Know your demographic and financial data and act on it. Speak the language of business and use it to build opportunities and wealth. I attended a recent business presentation by a local television station on the importance of baby boomer women as the new power consumer. It was an impressive presentation in which they emphasized that they would be focusing on targeting their programing around this important demographic. Guess what? They did not have one single woman on their presentation team. The term tone deaf comes to mind.

Spending our money at businesses owned by women will start to have an impact on a company's bottom-line. These are all great solutions; however, we women need to put ourselves in the position to seize opportunities. Consider what areas might be a fit for our brand and do it.

7. Go Big and Bold! Blaze a Trail!

Start a movement! Become a contrarian! Differentiate! Disrupt! Build a tribe! Stay connected and be relevant. Transform your vision of what future you want for you and your family.

8. Create Your Own Public Relations Team.

Speak up on social media or form your own TV channel. As New York senator Kirsten E. Gillibrand says, "Don't sit back and wait for the system to change, be instruments of change."

Support women and female issues by supporting candidates for office at every level. Influence the political discourse by running for political office or supporting candidates with pro-women agendas or by taking a leadership role in grassroots organizations. But that's another book.

9. Build Community and Business Leadership.

Join and take on a leadership position with a business or non-profit board of directors, get exposed to corporate decision-makers, and sponsor events in the community. I chair the South Florida Business Leadership Network, a business-to-business board focused on educating employers about the benefits for hiring disabled employees. Women in leadership positions must educate and hold accountable our male colleagues and ourselves. It will take all of us and 100% of our effort to solve this problem.

The above suggestions became the basis for the second edition of this book. You will learn more information on how to change policy and create your own movement in chapter 7.

Jamaica Leads the World in Proportion of Women Managers

The International Labor Organization reports that Jamaica, at 59.3%, tops both the United States and United Kingdom in percentage of women managers.

I am proud to share that my three audacious sisters in Jamaica number among the women leaders the study references.

My Trailblazing Sisters

Andree Nembhard re-branded herself as a certified executive coach in 2002. She is certified through the International Coach Federation (ICF). Andree founded and serves as president of Roxana Consulting, a successful leadership coaching and training firm in Kingston Jamaica. She is also a lecturer of Transformational Leadership at the Mona School of Business, the University of the West Indies in Jamaica.

Patricia Scott has been involved in industrial development projects for most of her career. She has enjoyed an impressive career with the National Investment Bank of Jamaica, the Caribbean Development Bank, and the United Nations Industrial Development Agency (UNIDO) for more than 30 years; all while implementing projects in member countries in Latin America, the Caribbean, Africa, and Asia. Currently retired, Patricia stays active as a philanthropist and a member of the U.N. Women's Guild.

Sandra Scott, Deputy Director of Tourism for the Government of Jamaica for over three years, is responsible for marketing Jamaica to the world. She is frequently featured and honored for her impressive results—attracting unprecedented numbers of tourists to Jamaica. Previously, while serving as Regional Director in Canada for the Jamaica Tourist Board, Canada moved from the number three position to number two for visitor arrivals to Jamaica.

The U.S., at 49%, is ranked 15th in the world. This, in spite of the fact that, "An increasing number of studies are also demonstrating positive links between women's participation in top decision-making teams and structures and business performance. But there is a long way to go before we achieve true gender equality in the workplace, especially when it comes to top management positions," the report added.[10]

We have all the qualities to catapult ahead. All we need is the confidence, a compelling brand, and a powerful image. We must take action on all fronts, use our mammoth spending power to pressure companies to promote women to C-level positions, and accelerate and grow our entrepreneurship ventures.

As *The Economist* indicates, "female empowerment is the most profound social change of our times."

Let's get out front and lead that change!

CHAPTER 7 -
THE AUDACITY TO DISRUPT THE STATUS QUO

"Go Big and Bold! Blaze a Trail! Start a movement! Disrupt! Differentiate! Transform your vision of what you want for you and your family."
~ Pamela and Tamara Toussaint

Sexual abuse, harassment, and other disempowering behaviors came to a head within our society in the latter half of 2017. Both women and men in government, media, entertainment, and corporate America have endured sexual harassment, bullying, and other indignities for the sake of careers and livelihoods, while self-confidence has steadily been eroded and prosperity threatened.

Rich and powerful women, from politicians to news anchors to Hollywood actors, have had enough abuse and are speaking up, leading to a tidal wave of high-level abusers, primarily male, being exposed and fired from their once lucrative positions.

However, everyday women who depend on

their paychecks, husbands' salaries, or family support to survive are still silenced by fear.

- What will they do if they speak up to their bosses?
- What will happen if they report the abuse to HR or another person in power?
- What if they are retaliated against or lose their jobs?

Now that it exists, what will these women (and the few men) do with the global #MeToo and #TimesUp movements? Nothing? Continue to suffer? Not options!

These people are our targeted *Audacity to Disrupt* audience!

Speak Up & Take Action

In her acceptance speech at the 2018 Golden Globes award ceremony, actress Laura Dern said, "Speaking out without the fear of retribution is our new Northstar."

Speaking up and out is, indeed, the first step. We must courageously turn up the heat, take control, turn the tide, and transform our society once and for all.

I applaud how the Women's Marches are inspiring the next bold step for individuals—getting women and enlightened men to vote for change and run for office. These change agents are using social media to create a movement using #PowertothePolls as a call to action. They are also providing women with the tools and resources to do even more by utilizing the EmilysList website[1] that enhances and increases the reach of social media. The results already are dramatic. Women are running for political office in record numbers, while male and female candidates, with any hint of a questionable reputation, are being rejected.

Tactical and Strategic Solutions

There is no better time for the Audacious Woman to disrupt the status quo and lay out a plan to transform and co-create prosperity. I am proposing a two-phase solution—a short-term tactical response and a long-term strategic approach.

First, we have to deal with the current problem, take care of the abused and vulnerable women and men who are being harassed and bullied. At the same time, we will work on a long-term solution building a strong foundation and an education and empowerment network, to ensure that women and men are empowered to pursue careers, and both lead and live prosperous lives.

Short-Term Tactical Response

The tactical approach provides employees with ideas and resources to take action if they are in an abusive situation or expect that their workplace is likely to become toxic.

To be clear, we are not proposing to offer advice or legal support. We recommend that you refer those issues to the proper resources, as suggested.

1. Know Your Rights in the Workplace.

As a former Human Resources leader, I am calling on my fellow HR leaders to take control and lead transformation in this area. It's not enough to just update the policies. As an employee, you must know what constitutes harassment, discrimination, and abuse. Have you been trained in sexual harassment or hostile workplace policies? If not, contact your Human Resources department to get clarification. While you are there, ask them to explain the process they follow.

The harassment policy of Palm Beach State College, where I teach, is very well written, with a clear outline of how to identify harassment and what to do about it.

2. What to do if you are harassed?

Do not ignore any signs of harassment. It breaks my heart to hear the story about the young U.S. Olympic gymnasts who were abused for years by the team doctor. They reported the incidents, but the adults did not listen. The doctor was sentenced to well over 100 years in prison for the abuse, which has caused vast and irreparable damage to the young ladies.

If the "adults" do not listen, go a step higher than your boss and HR, and document every interaction. File a formal complaint. Call your mentor.

Take note that the abuse does not always happen between a male and female. A manager shared on LinkedIn that enduring abusive treatment by her female boss led to serious health problems and a leave of absence at the insistence of her physician.

3. Speak out about your experience.

What we are proposing, however, takes guts. You could lose your job and financial security if you speak up or blow the whistle. But a toxic workplace takes its toll. You must weigh the risk and **seek legal counsel** before taking any action.

4. Do not sign anything.

If you are fired for blowing the whistle on harassment or abuse, do not sign any documents, even something such as a confidentiality agreement, without approval of your attorney.

The above short-term tactics are just stopgap measures. Real change will come from a more defined and strategic approach.

Long-Term Strategic Approach

The Global Audacious Empowerment Network (GAEN, pronounced "gain") is a confidential empowerment zone where real transformation takes place. Women and men are prepared mentally, spiritually, and professionally to change the culture. We are a strong, empowered force focused on growth and prosperity. We are also prepared to audaciously address any potential abuse head-on until we root it out of our system worldwide and help restore the confidence and dignity of the abused.

GAEN begins with core members to lay the foundation using a "secret group" within Facebook in creating and collaborating with existing, local groups for women and men to meet and share ideas and strategies for effective transformation. For example, I belong to a local professional women's forum in West Palm Beach where we help each other grow professionally, expand our sphere of influence, and assist women to get out of homelessness and become self-sufficient once again.

GAEN will focus on training and coaching on empowerment, leadership, empathy, civility, emotional intelligence, presence, and confidence-building for entrepreneurs and those in traditional careers.

Who is invited to join GAEN? From college students to baby boomers, from every profession to every work-at-home mom.

The **Personal Branding Guide**—a gift in return for your purchase, and where the download link can be found later in this book—is the network's ultimate toolkit. But before you receive the personal branding guide, below is a list of ways for you to get started now thinking on your long-term strategy:

1. **Request to join the "secret" GAEN Facebook group.**

   Anyone committed to learning the tools of empowerment to stamp out sexual harassment, abuse, and other personal violations, is welcome to join. To ensure we make a great team, you will be required to answer a short questionnaire. The group administrators will review your application and respond accordingly. (The group link can be found in the personal branding guide.)

2. **Create a Powerful Personal Brand.**

   As Amy Cuddy says in her book, *Presence: Bringing Your Boldest Self to Your Biggest Challenges*[2], "Presence emerges when we feel personally powerful."

   Oprah Winfrey has a way of walking onto the stage with presence and commanding her audience's attention. During the 2018 Golden Globe Awards, she passionately issued a "call to action" supporting the #TimesUp movement that has "the desire to support women, men, people of color, and the LGBT community who have less access to media platforms and funds to speak up about harassment."[3] We were riveted when Oprah said, "No more" to the injustices.

Is she an expert on harassment issues? Perhaps. Just the sheer force of her presence, however, convinced many that she would be a good candidate for the president of the United States of America.

Although we cannot guarantee you will become Oprah—or the president—we will guide you in developing the same self-confidence and ability to inspire transformation.

3. You, Incorporated: Develop a Business Plan for your Career/Life.

As an entrepreneur, you know that you can't run your businesses without a plan. It takes vision and preparation. You see yourself personally, career-wise and financially, where you will be in 5 or 7 years. Make sure you share the plan with a trusted friend or mentor. As an entrepreneur or an employee, this activity will position you to confidently take control of your career and financial situation and prepare you for any unplanned job upheaval.

I was invited by the college where I teach to lead the "Foundations of Leadership" training for staff and faculty. We just finished the 6-month program and held the graduation ceremony. It was amazing to observe the growth and confidence the participants exhibited, and the bonding and peer coaching that resulted.

Two of the women graduates told me that I inspired them so much to transform their mindset and careers that they already applied for advanced degrees, and one had re-enrolled to complete her Bachelors!

If you don't have one yet, I highly recommend creating a plan encompassing the remainder of the year. In case I haven't mentioned it, using the personal branding guide will help you set up a well-defined action plan.

4. Maximize Women's Economic and Political Power.

As *The Economist* also says: "Women's economic empowerment is the most profound social change of our time." A significant part of the struggle why women are enduring abuse is that they need their jobs to survive; they don't have control of their finances and career. Start creating your "Plan A" life which you will develop in the personal branding guide. You can accomplish this while you continue your current job. Refer to the stories and examples of women in this book who successfully created a "Plan A" life and prospered.

5. Build Entrepreneurship Skills.

The decision to learn entrepreneurial skills whether you plan to start a business or not is a wise must-do. The entrepreneurial mindset is valued in corporate jobs. It has an element of creativity, risk-taking, and confidence.

Some of the skills to develop are ones that you may already have but need to strengthen. These include but are not limited to the:

- **Discipline** to stay on task to work both in and on your business
- **Vision** it takes to stay on top of the current marketplace and your competitors

- **Courage** to change things up when necessary, regardless if it's to pull back or ramp up

Together these skills will flex all your muscles to strengthen your mindset and knowledge, ensuring your success.

6. Develop Deal-Making Skills.

You may require start-up or venture capital (VC) to help your business get off the ground and grow. Did you know that women entrepreneurs only get just a little over 2% of the venture capital dollars available?[4]

Harvard Business School recently discovered that women and men get asked a series of different questions while seeking venture capital funding for their business.[5] Who knew?

So, what does it take to launch a VC or access other money? The GAEN community will provide or refer these resources to ensure you get access to all the venture capital necessary to get you off on the right foot.

We must think big. There is a lot of money that is ready to be spent, but so few women and people of color are in a position to take advantage of the assistance. Why? Because no one has told them these resources exist, and traditionally, we have not been confident in discussing our needs and laying out a compelling case for potential investors to fund our business ventures.

GAEN aims to change that.

Legacy of Self-Confidence, Audacity and Courage

What will we tell our children and grandchildren about this—or any— time of disruption and what we did about it?

At the time I originally wrote the book, I challenged my readers and workshop and book-signing participants to visualize their ideal future. What will your future be?

To leave behind a legacy, one of which you will be proud, you must move from your vision to actualizing that transformation journey.

Dear men and women, this is your opportunity to co-create a world where we can all prosper. As Coca-Cola Chairman and CEO Muhtar Kent says, "You have to be constructively discontent and resolutely focused on your future."

We have begun to disrupt the status quo; we are exercising our collective power to transform the world for generations to come.

What will be your next step?

CHAPTER 8 -
BUILD IT BEFORE YOU NEED IT

> *"Relationships are all there is. Everything in the universe only exists because it is in relationship to everything else. Nothing exists in isolation. We have to stop pretending we are individuals that can go it alone."*
>
> ~ Margaret Wheatley

Our *Ultimate Image Coach* team hosts *Pop of Color Holiday Networking Reception* around Christmas each year. The idea was to put a different, fun, and Caribbean spin on the serious business of networking, encouraging everyone to get dressed up in festive holiday attire, enjoy Caribbean cuisine and music, and forge serious, strategic partnerships and friendships. It has become the event that business women and men look forward to every December.

"Pop of Color was an amazing and fun networking event, we loved the ambience, festive mood, dressing up, food, but most important, we made great business connections,

I am now partnering with a person I met there on an entrepreneurial venture."
~ Anonymous Networker at the *Ultimate Image Coach's* Annual *Pop of Color Holiday Networking Reception*

What is networking? One definition is when you interact with other people to exchange information and develop contacts, especially, to further your career.[1]

Networking is also described as oxygen for your business. Without it, your business is simply a hobby.

Know, Like, and Trust

Remember, people do business with people they know, like, and trust. Finding opportunities for your business will only happen if you network. It's all about building relationships and partnerships, yet these take time to nurture. Networking helps to authenticate your business as real. People want to know you personally so they can begin the process of building trust. They want to make sure your image conveys—and is consistent with—the brand you build online.

Technology and the mobile revolution were supposed to catapult us to fame and unprecedented fortune, but it has also eroded our ability to communicate effectively.

I call myself a serial networker for good reason. I am where I am because I have built and nurtured my business network from Chicago to Princeton to Fort Lauderdale, Atlanta, West Palm Beach, Washington D.C., Jamaica, and beyond.

Build It Before You Need It

In his book, *Never Eat Alone*—and one of my favorite authors on the power of networking—Keith Ferrazzi says:

> *"I've come to believe that connecting is one of the most important business—and life—skill sets you'll ever learn. Why? Because, flat out, people do business with people they know and like."* [2]

I mentioned in chapter 1 that building strategic, reciprocal relationships are key transformational tools. I want to echo what I said earlier.

Relationships are being forged at networking events, all the while job seekers are checking employment postings online, and entrepreneurs are cold-calling. Personal relationships lead to unprecedented opportunities—for instance, speaking engagements, volunteer, and contract gigs. This is the *Hidden Job Market*. You must be consistently visible and generous with your network. Within my strategic networking workshops, the main point I emphasize is that building solid relationships is the most critical part of a successful transformation journey.

So why do so many people resist networking? Many do so because of their personality. They claim to not be sociable, they are introverts, and, if they are in transition, they are in a hurry to find a new job. They just want to dispense with all the networking stuff and find a contact, get a job. Reality check—this is not how the world works.

In workshops, I use my son's networking demeanor as an example. He is a natural conversationalist. He walks into a business or social event and engages easily in conversation. His confident style causes others to gravitate to him. This is the type of effortless networking skill that opens doors for further career or opportunity discussions.

Plan Your Strategic Networking Activities

You are planning to attend a huge industry conference, with upwards of 5,000 attendees. Plan to get the most out of it. Below are six tips to help make your networking experience an enjoyable and profitable experience:

- **Research.** Study the event's agenda and list of speakers and invited guests. Review their biographies on LinkedIn or "Google" them. List the guests you want to meet and why, such as strategic partner, job search, and potential customer. Try to find any linkage with the contacts you are targeting, such as organization membership, alumni organizations, and hobbies.

- **Plan.** Like any project, planning will give you the competitive edge. Create a spreadsheet with names and reason for meeting; prioritize into an A-list (must meet, think prospect, strategic partner) and B-list (nice to know, potential strategic partner).

- **Radiate.** Get plenty of rest, arrive dressed to impress, and wear comfortable shoes. It takes about three seconds to make a lasting first impression (you want to make a great one!), and this is a critical part of your strategy. A superbly fitting power suit or dress in your favorite power color is a must. By all means wear a favorite piece of statement accessory (jewelry, purse, or belt) or any other accent to your professional outfit that could be a great ice-breaker or conversation starter. Get ready to have all eyes on you.

- **Deliver.** Make sure your elevator pitch is crisp and natural and have 2-3 key questions you can tailor to ask each A- and B-list contact. While you are speaking with the contact, write on the back of their business card—in short hand—anything that helps you with following up with them. For example, if the contact would be a great customer for your business, write "C" on the back of his card; if she would be a good strategic partner, write "SP"; job search, "JS", etc.

- **Move Along.** Remember to not get stuck talking to one person the entire conference, yet also make sure you give that person your full attention, and not look as if you are ready to flee to the next person or group. You should spend no more than 2-3 minutes per person, with an extra 1-2 minutes with A-list contacts. Resist the temptation to be too sociable. Most importantly, you are in command. Stay focused.

- **Follow Up.** As soon as you return from your networking session, review your progress to see how you did with your A-list. Follow-up is critical. Send out follow-up emails within 48 hours, invite key contacts to join your LinkedIn network, and have a plan for staying in touch. Share something useful, like an article or a blog or a referral.

Executing these simple steps on a consistent basis will increase your strategic network and create unlimited business opportunities.

EPILOGUE - LOVE, LAUGH, PROSPER!

"Whatever we see as our 'gift' or 'direction for the future' becomes strengthened once we find a Supportive Someone who is willing to reinforce and believe in our vision."
~ Marilyn Murray Willison, *The Self-Empowered Woman*[1]

If it's Tuesday, It's got to Be Zumba

My family, friends, and close business associates know I am passionate about Zumba. If you haven't heard of Zumba, it's a lively and exhilarating combination of international music of all kinds with exercise. I so enjoy it and rarely accept invitations for Tuesday evenings because I get an amazing surge of energy and happiness from dancing Zumba.

If you could imagine a life filled with joy…. what would it feel or look like?

The more my friends, family, clients and I talk about it, we are all seeking the same thing:

prosperity, balance, and well-being. We all want to make our lives a testament to our sacrifices and hard work.

Healthy Employees... Healthy Bottom-Line

I can't tell you how many of my close professional friends and family members have nearly ruined their health and happiness by chasing corporate and financial success. No wonder stress, burnout, and depression are rampant among working women.

As a corporate HR leader for many years, I was painfully aware of the human and financial cost of stress in the workplace. Most of the sick days taken by employees are stress-related. In her book, *Thrive*, Arianna Huffington wrote such illnesses result in 105 million workdays lost each year.[2]

I count my blessings. I have never been healthier—body, spirit, and soul. I still reflect on the day when I left my corporate job and started my business—this had been my personal liberation and renewal day.

Focus on Health and Well-Being

I love the safety announcements we get on airplanes before take-off. They tell us to put on our own oxygen masks before helping others. Well, use that advice in life. We must take care of ourselves first, and then we can help those around us.

Women in careers are juggling at unprecedented rates. It becomes even more intense if they are parents, taking care of family members, in a low paid job, working two jobs, or struggling with student loans or other debt. Several of my college students have told me in the last few years that they had to take a semester or an entire year off due to financial burdens; they either had to pay back loans or work enough to cover bills at home. Both my hair stylist and esthetician work countless hours to make the rent and other household bills.

Focus on you! In whatever limited time and means you may have, start the day with at least 15 minutes of "me time." Meditate, be still, eat a healthy breakfast, and exercise. Walk your dog, dance, run, walk, bike, or Zumba. This practice will get your day off to a great start. It will make a world of difference in your health and happiness. And then, end your day with more meditation, being still, or writing in a journal on what happened during the day, and any new ideas or moments of inspiration.

Turn it Off

"The average smart phone user checks his or her device every six and a half minutes. That works out to around 150 times per day. Our brains are naturally wired to connect. There is evidence that it can begin to rewire our brains to make us less adept at real human connection."
~ Arianna Huffington, *Thrive*[3]

I recently heard several young women joking that they sleep with their smart phone next to their pillows and check it every time it pings. Use these devices to help you simplify your life, not consume your life. Do not react to every ring, text, or email. Schedule time during your day when you will focus on each of these activities and stay true to your schedule.

Love

Reverend Taylor Stevens, Unity of the Palm Beaches, said it best:

> *"Love is not just a mental concept...It is a living truth."*

Our family is living proof of that statement. As I shared earlier in the book, even though my siblings and I have been hundreds or thousands of miles apart, we have a strong love for each other that transcends cities, nations and continents. We are there (sometimes virtually) to share in the successes and joys and are supportive and attentive in those moments of need. Love conquers all. We burn up email, phone lines, Skype, and Zoom! Above everything else in this book, this is the legacy I hope we hand off to the next generations, and a key lesson to share with those who embark on this transformation journey.

Live Life

I am sure you, your family and friends frequently say that life is short. We should enjoy every moment. Let's stop talking about it and just live it. I took that to heart. My husband and I have been sprinkling in a cruise here and there, spending a lot of time with family, playing dominoes and dancing with our huge fun-loving family, my husband's siblings and their families. Our friends know that they do not need to guess where we will be on Sunday afternoons. We will be at our usual huge Sunday family dinner in Miramar, Florida. But that's another book. We love and enjoy our family and friends! There is no greater compliment than to hear our children, family, and friends tell us that they want to live a life like ours when they grow up. It is not an opulent life, but it is a rich, blessed life.

Leave a Trail

> *"Do not follow where the path may lead… Go instead where there is no path and leave a trail."*
>
> ~ Anonymous

I end where I started. This journey would not have been possible without the sacrifices, vision, and mentoring by **my mother**. Building on that amazing foundation, I had so many mentors, coaches, friends—too numerous to mention—who helped me become the person I am today. We are blessed to have male leaders, family members who support us and encourage us to stretch ourselves beyond what we think is possible.

As Senator Warren once said, "We didn't get there on our own." Someone mentored, coached, supported, or provided a bridge or a shoulder. I can think of countless corporate mentors—male and female—who mentored me, and without whose support I would not have achieved my life's goals. We owe nothing less to our children and grandchildren, who will become the next generations of women and men.

Remember Yolanda, Susan, and Bonnie?

In this book's prologue, I shared their stories with you. Here's an update. Yolanda started a business after resigning. She is doing well. Although she has experienced some financial bumps along the way, Yolanda has become very creative managing her budget and doing more targeted marketing. Remember, this is a marathon, and I am convinced that she will hang in there for the long haul.

Susan remains unemployed. She is dabbling in project work while she continues to look for a "permanent" job. She is doing a lot more networking and building solid, strategic partnership relationships. Susan is teaching part-time at the local college and finds that she enjoys the academic environment.

Bonnie is still struggling with being the only female executive on the management committee. However, I have worked with her on developing executive presence and gravitas skills, and is making good progress. Plus, she is asserting herself more effectively in meetings. Bonnie is now mentoring female mid-level managers who are in line for senior leadership positions.

So Where Do You Go From Here?

Have you had your "Click Moment"? Here are some ideas. Vary your network. Interact with people you would not normally interact with. You are not going to find those moments if you keep circulating in the same groups exclusively. I make it a point to vary my network with art fairs, church, women's groups, and non-profit events, just to name a few. Of course, I network with students of all demographics. My *Ultimate Image Coach* team members are millennial professional women—and boy, do I learn from them! These experiences have opened my world to the challenges and opportunities that millennial women offer. It gets me thinking of ways to connect dots, create linkages and solve problems in new and exciting ways.

I urge and challenge every woman to encourage and mentor a younger woman and man, a teen or pre-teen, to dream big, use an active imagination, be confident and polished, poised and powerful, to develop collaborative working relationships and support systems. They are our future leaders. This will make a difference.

While helping other women individually to become an Audacious Woman, you will Blaze Your Own Path to Prosperity.

A Gift for You to Say Thanks

Because you first invested in yourself by purchasing this book, or if it had been given to you, we, at Ultimate Image Coach would like to help even more.

Please go to http://bit.ly/pamt2018 to download a free personal branding guide that, with this book, will assist you in creating the Plan A life you were meant to live.

ABOUT THE AUTHORS

Pamela Toussaint, MBA, is a personal branding consultant, corporate trainer, author and keynote speaker. She is an Image Consultant and Career Transition Expert.

Founder of *Ultimate Image Coach*, Toussaint works with companies, career changers, and universities wishing to provide members with a competitive advantage, personal branding, effective communication, polished and powerful presence, customer service, professional workplace skills, and business acumen.

As a professor at Palm Beach State College, Toussaint works with students to build critical human and customer relations skills in preparation for successful careers.

Toussaint's corporate leadership experience spans four decades. Serving as a Human Resource executive and senior client relationship leader with Fortune 500 corporations, she earned a reputation as a passionate leader and developer of high-performance teams.

She is a member of HR Palm Beach County and the Chamber of Commerce of the Palm Beaches.

Toussaint was born in Jamaica and moved to West Palm Beach, FL in 2005 after living in Chicago, Illinois and Bucks County, Pennsylvania. She and husband Gabriel, married for over 40 years, love to travel, cruise, read, and dance. She has two children and four grandchildren.

With over 10 years of experience in the legal industry in New York, Miami, Atlanta and now Washington D.C., **Tamara Toussaint, JD**, currently works in Account Management for the world's leading source of intelligent information for businesses and professionals.

Toussaint uses her background in diversity, the legal industry, and higher education to provide practical, professional presence consulting to young professionals and those in a mid-career makeover through *Ultimate Image Coach,* an image consulting and personal branding company, she co-owns with her mother. Toussaint has delivered speeches and workshops on diversity issues, executive presence and the importance of a professional image for Georgia Diversity Council, National Black

MBA Association, Alabama State University, Palm Beach State College, *Walker's Legacy* and New Leaders Council. Her specialty is coaching clients on online personal branding, communication skills, interview preparation, social media branding, and professional attire for every occasion. She helps businesses, executives, and politicians create and execute a consistent online and personal presence which gives them a critical competitive advantage.

Toussaint is currently serving her 4th year as a member of The White House Commission on Presidential Scholars. She has a Juris Doctor degree from the University of Miami School of Law, and Bachelor of Arts degree in history, with a minor in French, from the University of Michigan.

CONNECT WITH PAMELA & TAMARA

Website
http://www.ultimateimagecoach.com

Facebook
http://www.facebook.com/ultimateimagecoach

Google+
https://plus.google.com/+PamelaToussaintUltimateImageCoach

https://plus.google.com/+Ultimateimagecoach1

LinkedIn
http://www.linkedin.com/in/pamelatoussaint

https://www.linkedin.com/in/tamaratoussaint

Twitter
https://twitter.com/ImagecoachPamT

YouTube
https://www.youtube.com/user/UltimageImageCoach

Ultimate Image Coach
We Polish...You Shine

REFERENCE & READING LIST

Prologue

1. Cook, Blanche Wiesen. Eleanor Roosevelt, Volume One 1884-1933. Penguin; Reprint edition, 1993.

2. The Council of Economic Advisers, Nine Facts About American Families And Work, June 2014.

3. Sandberg, Sheryl. Lean In. Knopf, 1 edition, 2013.

4. Katty, Kay and Claire Shipman, The Confidence Code. Harper Business, 2014.

5. Huffington, Arianna. Thrive., New York: Harmony Books, 2014.

Chapter 1

6. http://www.forbes.com/sites/susanadams/2014/06/20/most-americans-are-unhappy-at-work/

7. Johannson, Franz. The Click Moment. Portfolio Hardcover, 2012.

Chapter 2

1. Hill, Napoleon Jeremy P. Tarcher. Think and Grow Rich. New York: Penguin, a member of the Penguin Group (USA) Inc., 2010.

2. http://www.variety.com/2015/tv/news/ann-curry-to-depart-nbc-news-1201404102/

3. http://vitals.nbcnews.com/_news/2013/02/07/16889472-millennials-are-the-most-stressed-out-generation-new-survey-finds

4. http://www.she-conomy.com/facts-on-women

5. Ambani, Dhirubhai. Against All Odds: A Story Of Courage, Perseverance And Hope. Tata: McGraw-Hill, 2008.

Chapter 3

1. Godin, Seth. Purple Cow: Transform Your Business by Being Remarkable. Portfolio, 2003.

2. Csikszentmihalyi, Mihaly. Concept of Flow--Human Relations: Strategies For Success. New York: McGraw Hill Education, 2014.

3. http://www.TheRealHaiti.com

4. http://www.WalkersLegacy.com/

5. http://www.linkedin.com/in/MichelleDiffenderfer

Chapter 4

1. Gage, Randy. Risky is the New Safe. John Wiley & Sons, Inc., 2013.

2. DeGeneres, Ellen. Seriously…I'm Kidding. New York: Grand Central Publishing, 2011.

3. Schawbel, Dan. Me 2.0. Kaplan Publishing, 2014

4. Vaynerchuk, Gary. Crush It. Harper Studio; First Edition, 1st Printing edition, 2009.

5. http://www.forbes.com/sites/keldjensen/2012/04/12/intelligence-is-overrated-what-you-really-need-to-succeed/

Chapter 5

1. Blount, Jeb. People Buy You. New Jersey: John Wiley & Sons, Inc., 2010.

2. http://www.forbes.com/sites/meghancasserly/2012/12/10/the-10-skills-that-will-get-you-a-job-in-2013/

3. http://www.qz.com/87154/emotional-intelligence-is-a-better-predictor-of-success-than-iq/

4. http://www.nonverbalgroup.com/2011/08/how-much-of-communication-is-really-nonverbal/

5. http://www.prweb.com/releases/2012/10/prweb10050433.htm

6. http://www.harpersbazaar.com/culture/features/confident-moves-to-master

7. Janke, Christine. The Well-Spoken Woman. New York: Promethius Books, 2011.

Chapter 6

1. Katty, Kay and Claire Shipman, The Confidence Code. Harper Business, 2014.

2. http://www.forbes.com/sites/katebrodock/2013/05/06/women-in-leadership-as-an-economic-imperative/

3. http://www.businessinsider.com/container-store-ceo-kip-tindell-leadership-women-success-2014-10

4. http://www.catalyst.org/knowledge/women-ceos-sp-500

5. Gobe, Mark. Emotional Branding. New York: Allworth Press, 2010.

6. http://www.dol.gov/equalpay/

7. Sandberg, Sheryl. Lean In. Knopf, 1 edition, 2013.

8. The Council of Economic Advisers, Nine Facts About American Families And Work, June 2014.

9. The Council of Economic Advisers, Nine Facts About American Families And Work, June 2014.

10. http://www.jamaicaobserver.com/news/Jamaica-has-highest-percentage-of-women-managers-globally---ILO-report

Chapter 7

1. https://www.emilyslist.org/

2. Cuddy, Amy, Presence: Bringing Your Boldest Self to Your Biggest Challenges, Little, Brown and Company, 2015

3. https://en.wikipedia.org/wiki/Time%27s_Up_(movement)

4. http://fortune.com/2017/03/13/female-founders-venture-capital/

5. https://hbr.org/2017/06/male-and-female-entrepreneurs-get-asked-different-questions-by-vcs-and-it-affects-how-much-funding-they-get

Chapter 8

1. http://www.Google.com

2. Ferrazzi, Keith. Never Eat Alone. New York: Crown Business, 2014.

Epilogue

1. Murray-Wilson, Marilyn. The Self-Empowered Woman. BookSurge Publishing, 2009

2. Huffington, Arianna. Thrive. New York: Harmony Books, 2014.

3. Huffington, Arianna. Thrive. New York: Harmony Books, 2014.

www.ingramcontent.com/pod-product-compliance
Lightning Source LLC
Chambersburg PA
CBHW052258220526
45471CB00001B/398